Jenni Murray has been the regular presenter of Radio 4's *Woman's Hour* since 1987. In the Queen's Birthday Honours 1999 she was awarded an OBE for radio broadcasting. Jenni is the author of *The Woman's Hour*, a history of women since World War II and also the acclaimed *Is it me, or is it hot in here?*. She contributes to numerous newspapers and magazines and is an occasional documentary film-maker. She lives with her partner and two sons in London and Cheshire.

Also by Jenni Murray
and available from Vermilion:

Is it me, or is it hot in here?

That's My Boy!

*A modern parent's guide
to raising a happy and
confident son*

Jenni Murray

Vermilion
LONDON

3 5 7 9 10 8 6 4 2

Text copyright © Jenni Murray 2003

Jenni Murray has asserted her right to be identified as the author of this
work in accordance with the Copyright, Designs and Patents Act, 1988.

First published in 2003 by Vermilion,
an imprint of Ebury Press,
Random House,
20 Vauxhall Bridge Road,
London SW1V 2SA
www.randomhouse.co.uk

Random House Australia (Pty) Limited
20 Alfred Street, Milsons Point, Sydney,
New South Wales 2061, Australia

Random House New Zealand Limited
18 Poland Road, Glenfield,
Auckland 10, New Zealand

Random House South Africa (Pty) Limited
Endulini, 5A Jubilee Road,
Parktown 2193, South Africa

The Random House Group Limited Reg. No. 954009

Papers used by Vermilion are natural, recyclable products
made from wood grown in sustainable forests.

Printed and bound in Great Britain by
Clays Ltd, St Ives plc

A CIP catalogue record for this book
is available from the British Library

ISBN 0-09-188964-2

CONTENTS

INTRODUCTION

I chose the title of this book with some trepidation, fearing it would infuriate number two son, Charlie, now fifteen. It's a reminder of one of the more embarrassing moments he suffered as a result of having an over-enthusiastic mother with a big mouth and a voice to match. He was twelve or thirteen at the time and (this is not pride talking, it's a fact) a leading light in his school rugby team.

Now, I've never liked rugby and can't for one second comprehend why it's currently the fastest growing and most popular sport among girls after football, but, there you go, times, they are a changing. To me it's dirty, wet, cold, violent and potentially lethally dangerous, but I have dutifully stood on the touchline week after week, wearing my thermals, learning that you get five for a try and two for a conversion, trying to distinguish a ruck from a scrum from a maul or working out why they've been given a line out (one friend from the *Woman's Hour* office tells me she got terribly anxious when her son came home and proudly announced he was going to be a hooker!). I've grudgingly acknowledged that it's a highly skilled game which teaches generosity and team spirit, uses up huge amounts of energy, and keeps the guys fit and off the streets.

So, on this particular day, he picked up the ball at the twenty-two (that, for the uninitiated, is about three-quarters of the way into the other side's half) and ran like a demon, ducking and weaving to dodge the tackles, triumphantly placing the ball directly between the posts behind his team's try line, perfectly positioned to give the kicker the best shot at goal.

And it just slipped out. Hard as I try not to be one of those awful pushy parents who demonise the ref and grunt 'Go on my son', I couldn't resist yelling those three fatal words: 'That's My Boy!'. Ecstatic maternal pride oozed from every syllable, which, of course, resounded the length and breadth of the pitch, and was heard by every single player, including mine own.

If looks could kill he would have been an instant orphan and no amount of apology or explanation after the match was accepted in mitigation. 'Do not, Mother, (it's Mum when he's not cross) ever humiliate me like that again!' was absolutely all he had to say on the matter and there it rested until now.

I decided to go with the title for two reasons. I had discussed it with Charlie who agreed it was OK to use as long he got a cut from the royalties. He must have absorbed with his mother's milk the family motto, which most journalists adopt, stolen from the American author and screenwriter, Nora Ephron: 'Life is copy'. It was, of course, vital to have his agreement and that of his brother, Ed, who's now twenty and at university, before I could even embark on this work, as it's their lives as well as my own that form its backbone. Suffice to say, it's costing me!

The second reason for the choice of title was its celebratory tone. This book was born out of anger at the demonisation of boys that's become common currency in the past decade or so. Only a few months ago, in February of 2003, the distinguished novelist Eva Figes, writing an article about the joys of being a grandmother, said with terrifying insouciance,

> *'I have always found that every one of my granddaughters is incredibly good when in my care. No tears, no tantrums . . . when I do lay down certain guidelines, about washing hands before lunch or whatever, they are always obeyed without question. The relationship is wonderfully conflict free. It might be a different story, of course, if one of my children had produced a boy.'*

How often do we hear about the trouble with boys, failing boys, difficult boys, bad boys, naughty boys, slugs, snails and puppy dogs' tails? Not an ounce of sugar, spice and all things nice, but when I looked at my two I saw nothing but fun, affection, a willingness to learn and an infinite capacity for hard work when it was called for. There was a grunty period and the occasional scrap that had to be mediated, but on the whole it's been a pleasure and they have been the light of my life.

That's not to say there are no difficult questions that need to be addressed. There are those who – convinced by evolutionary psychology and scientific experimentation which appears to demonstrate that male and female brains work differently – argue that men are from Mars and women from Venus, or that men can't talk and women can't read maps, or that men are natural hunter gatherers and it's in a woman's nature to be kind and caring. I'm afraid I think it's all nonsense and that our ambitions, talents, sensitivities and abilities are far more likely to be the product of social pressure and the atmosphere in which we are raised than of any genetic blueprint.

Feminism gave women the social support to reject the idea that we are at the mercy of our hormones and we've been afforded the opportunity and backup to determine our futures as individual human beings, rejecting the assumption that our natural milieu is in the kitchen or nursery. We were told it was indecent for a woman to dissect a corpse – now medical schools are training equal numbers of girls and boys to be doctors. We were told competing as athletes would ruin our chances of having children – tell that to Sally Gunnel and any number of other fast and powerful women who are also mothers. We were told it was unladylike for a woman to vote, let alone become Prime Minister. Margaret Thatcher would, I think, disagree.

Our choices need no longer be determined by our gender because we've accepted that there are all kinds of different women – from the violent to the gentle, the selfish to the caring, the ambitious to be out in the world to the content to be at home. But, what have we done to give our boys the same degree of choice? What support have they had in exploring the idea that there are as many ways of being masculine as there are of being feminine? Where's the fury at the suggestion that violence and anti-social behaviour are a man's lot because he's awash with testosterone, when the merest hint that PMT or the menopause turns the female brain to mush is brushed aside with the contempt it deserves?

A girl can wear trousers with impunity. David Beckham discovered to his cost that we are not yet ready to accept a man in a sarong or even a man who shows he's hurt. When his boss Sir Alex Ferguson kicked a football boot, which hit Beckham in the face and

cut his eyebrow, it was not Sir Alex who was censured for his petu-
lant and violent behaviour, but David for showing his wound. And
the insults, which were thrown at him, were those that strike a chill
in the heart of any masculine man. He was not a wuss, a wimp or a
baby, but a Big Girl's Blouse, under the thumb of his wife, Victoria.
Interesting that when men want to bring each other down they
imbue each other with feminine qualities.

Equally, the man who chooses to stay home and look after the
children (as mine did), because the woman seems better suited to
be career-oriented, is still regarded with some suspicion at the
school gate and finds that people at parties drift away when he
jokes that he makes the bread rather than winning it. The men of
his generation had to be very confident in their masculinity, and
preferably look, as mine does, like a front-row mean machine that
you wouldn't want to confront on a dark night, to get away with it.

Some people argue that what's been dubbed a crisis in masculinity
is the fault of feminism. Commentators like Melanie Phillips suggest
that the removal of the social stigma from around women who were
ready to earn their own living and bring up a child alone (because
they weren't prepared to bring up two babies – the man and the
child that resulted from the coupling) has absolved men from the
traditional responsibilities of supporting and remaining loyal to a
family – leaving them utterly lost. Professor James Tooley in his book
The Miseducation of Women goes so far as to say we've made a terrible
mistake in encouraging women to think they can compete on the
same level as men, because what they really want is a man to take
care of them and their children. Feminist education, he argues, gave
us a generation of Bridget Joneses.

It's my view that men and boys have not been absolved of
responsibility. Quite the reverse. They've been given more,
requiring them to work out, as girls have always had to do, how
they will juggle both work and family. Men will also have to accept
that to be fully rounded human beings – rather than despised and
power crazed patriarchal maniacs – they will have to acknowledge
that all members of the human race create a mess and need feeding,
and it's not the automatic responsibility of one sex to be house-
keeper to the other. If we don't manage to instil this in our sons, we

will simply create another generation where relationships are stretched to breaking point on the rack of mismatched expectation. As my mother would put it, 'Another generation of men who'll grow up to be a rod for some poor woman's back.'

Professor Tooley might be astonished at the number of non-Bridget Joneses who did get their man and their baby (the American feminist and author of *The Beauty Myth*, Naomi Wolf, among them) and who report how they discovered with shock that what they thought they'd married – an equal and a best friend – suddenly morphed into 'breadwinner who can't cook won't cook' once the babies came along. As the sociologist, Professor Jonathon Gershuny put it so elegantly, 'We've created what I call The Allerednic syndrome. It's Cinderella backwards. In the old days the Handsome Prince married a scullery maid and turned her into a princess. Now he marries a Princess and turns her into a scullery maid.'

Our boys are hungry for information and guidance on how they can fulfil the new demands being placed upon them. The writer and broadcaster Tariq Ali, who has two daughters and a son, summed up best how keen boys are to learn how to fit into the new world in which they are going to make their family lives:

'I think there is something pushing boys. They are searching for an image of what masculinity should be. In the absence of something complex and interesting and available and close, they look to the very shallow role models that we as a society provide for them: the things they see on television and all the beat up stuff on the computer games. We need to get together and start talking about how we bring up boys who are sensitive human beings.'

Quite.

This is not an academic tome. Where new research seems thorough and free of the political baggage which seeks, vainly in my view, to turn the clock back to an era where men were men and women knew their place, I have drawn upon it. But, as another Professor of Sociology, Laurie Taylor, and his son, Matthew Taylor, note in their book *What Are Children For?*, there's no shortage of 'experts advising parents on what they should and should not do to bring up their children safely, responsibly and successfully. A large proportion of these pronouncements is pious in tone and based on dubious scientific findings'. I'm afraid you have to be just a little suspicious of any science that suggests men are genetically incapable of doing the ironing because they just can't get their brains around it. They can fly to the moon, but can't press a collar? How very convenient and what absolute tosh.

I remember reading a book some years ago, called *Mapping the Mind*, which was full of fascinating pictures in glorious technicolour, demonstrating electrical activity in the brain and purporting to show that we are indeed in 'two minds'. The brain's two hemispheres do appear to have different functions. The right side of the brain is said to be connected with emotion. The right side is the one we need to survive at a basic level because it processes hunger, fear, love and aggression. The left side does sums and learns systems, it's the grey matter required to understand a train timetable. And, of course, there is a difference. More of the right brain lights up in a woman than in a man.

I laid a bet with a colleague. 'Just watch,' I said. 'I'll give it six months and this research will be used to support the theory that there are certain jobs for which women are not suited.' Sure enough, in less time than I predicted, came a report on equal opportunities in the fire service in Scotland. Here's what Neil Morrisson, then Her Majesty's Chief Inspector there, wrote in January 1999: 'Recent wide ranging research into the brain differences of males and females emphasises that males have advantages in solving manipulative and mathematical tasks. This would affect fire service operations such as pitching ladders, parking vehicles, sensing directions etc.'

Professor Susan Greenfield, a leading authority on the brain, warns against making assumptions based on its hard wiring. The brain, she says, is plastic and can change physically depending on its use, which accounts, presumably, for those female fire officers who were furious with Mr Morrison, as they can park a fire engine, pitch a ladder and find their way though a burning building with the best.

So, how do we deal with scientific theories that seem to shore up chauvinistic tendencies that limit all those men and women, boys and girls who just don't want to be put in boxes marked either 'suitable for males' or 'females only'? It's tempting to adopt the fascist solution of simply burning the offending material, but that's clearly not an option in a civilised environment. We can, though, always remind ourselves that science is far from perfect. It is performed by people who have right-brain emotions, beliefs and prejudices working alongside left-brain logic. So there are 'lies, damned lies and statistics'; as Nietzsche put it: 'There are no facts, only interpretations.'

This is a book that relies primarily on the experience of parents who recognise that their boys need new strategies to survive in the twenty-first century. In raising their sons, they've applied common sense, and a keen awareness that the gender balance has shifted, to the care of their boys, because, like me, they aimed to equip their sons with the knowledge that it's no longer good enough to emulate outdated models of what it means to be a man. These parents were also glad to contribute to that rare phenomenon – a celebration of sons.

CHAPTER ONE

IT'S A BOY!

For generations of women those three little words, 'It's a boy', heard at the end of their confinement brought a sense of enormous relief and pride in a job well done. If a woman managed to repeat the process, her status as a fecund mother of sons was assured. An heir and a spare – strong, healthy men who would fight for and protect her. They would carry on the dynasty, uphold the family name and feed and provide for her in old age. If, on the other hand, she brought forth only girls, she might at best be set aside or at worst despatched in favour of another brood mare with whom the lord and master might make further attempts to fulfil his paternal duty.

Henry VIII provides us with the best example of this quest for healthy male offspring. Divorced, beheaded, died, divorced, beheaded, survived! The fate of six women who succeeded between them in producing only two girls and one sickly boy. And, dammit, it was a girl who finally took up the royal reins and ruled for forty years of relative peace and prosperity. Elizabeth I did a jolly good job as queen with her declared 'heart and stomach of a man', but refused to marry or breed, more concerned with securing her own position than looking to the future. As a consequence she ended the Tudor line and opened the door for the only male heir around. James I of England and VI of Scotland was the son of the hated Scot, Mary, and ushered in a new royal dynasty, the Stuarts. Henry must have roared with fury in his grave. All his efforts to keep a Tudor on the throne had come to naught.

For those of us reproducing in the late twentieth and early

twenty-first centuries, in Western society at least, the gender land-scape into which our children are born is infinitely more complex.

The first hints that things had begun to change profoundly came in the late '90s when the journalist Alison Pearson wrote in the magazine *Having a Baby* in 1999: 'The sun is setting on sons these days. Girls are hot, girls are desirable, girls are the future. Holy mother, girls are the new boys.' She told how, in antenatal classes and maternity wards across the land, the days of parents taking pride in a son and heir were over, and claimed to detect 'an almost panicky craving for girls'. It led to a rash of articles in which parents, psychologists and experts in genetic manipulation were trotted out to extol the virtues of girls and the difficulties of raising boys – writer upon writer fell upon the old stereotypes.

In the *Sunday Times* in July 1999 Judith O'Reilly and Lois Jones quoted Linda Davies, a public relations consultant in London who was delighted when the midwives popped her baby onto her and said 'It's a girl'. Davies commented, 'You always have a daughter, but you can lose a son . . . Boys get married and leave their mothers, whilst daughters grow closer to their mothers as they grow up.' I really don't know what fantasy world she lives in. It seems rare now for a child of either gender to remain close to their parents as adults.

My anecdotal evidence suggests that women are often only too glad to break away from their mother's apron strings as they grow into adulthood, and are now deeply resentful of the assumption that it's a daughter's job to provide comfort and care for ageing parents, whilst sons can evade the responsibility. In the case of my own elder son, verging on adulthood at twenty, he feels a great desire to stay in touch with us now he's left home, with frequent phone calls and meetings, generally to ask for advice, share his enthusiasms or to be taken out for a decent meal. All of which seem perfectly proper reasons for a child of either sex to keep in touch with parents, but feeling duty bound to be on hand as best mate is nothing but a burdensome guilt trip.

It seems to me profoundly selfish, if not arrogant, to expect your children to become your friends. The generation gap seems too wide, and a parent's years-long role as provider and police officer is too often fraught with the conflicting messages of nurture and control ever to slide into the easy, undemanding atmosphere of friendship. We have to reconcile ourselves to the fact that it's our job to launch our children, boys and girls, into the world as rounded, confident human beings and not overwhelm them with a sense of their duty to become our best friends. They'll find those outside the family, as we did.

Linda Davies' husband, Grant Clark, a sports editor with the publisher Bloomberg, was quoted in the same article. 'I grew up with two brothers, so I know how nasty little boys can be. I haven't got a sister, so I think little girls are wonderful.' If only he'd had a little sister, then he'd have known, as all women do, that little girls are not necessarily so wonderful. It took feminism a long time to grow out of its insistence that women were, as the Canadian author Margaret Atwood put it, 'somehow gooder'. Or as the *Express* columnist Carol Sarler wrote early in 2003, 'Ten eleven-year-old boys were let loose in an old house for a Home Alone television experiment – and they trashed the place. Now, a year later, the project has been repeated with girls and the producers express astonishment that they destroyed nothing. Well, of course they didn't: girls would have been far too busy destroying each other!'

In the '60s and '70s, when the politics of sisterhood was at its height, it was a feminist heresy to claim that women were capable of violence or wickedness. The reaction to the Moors murderers, Ian Brady and Myra Hindley was typical. Although there was ample evidence that the crimes they committed against children were a joint enterprise, it was a commonly held belief that Brady was the bad lot and Hindley was simply a woman who had come under his spell and followed his instructions out of love and devotion.

It was not until Hindley died in 2002 that the full extent of her involvement was voiced and widely accepted. The feminist journalist Yvonne Roberts told the revealing story of a meeting she'd had with Hindley a decade earlier. Chris Tchaikovsky, another feminist who ran an organisation called Women in Prison, had taken Roberts to visit Hindley. Both fully expected to find that Hindley had been unfairly demonised as the embodiment of evil, but Roberts came away with the opposite impression. At one point in their interview Roberts asked Hindley how she could have picked up a child from the street in the evening and taken her to Brady, knowing what torture would ensue.

Hindley had replied with chilling lack of regret, 'She shouldn't have been out so late.' Roberts concluded that the woman, like Brady, was a psychopathic killer, clever enough to have read the feminist literature, which suggested women's crimes were generally due to abuse by or the malign influence of a man. It was her knowledge of these arguments and ability to articulate them, Roberts believed, that had led so many of Hindley's apologists, such as Lord Longford, to seek her release.

Atwood's novel *Cat's Eye*, published in the late '80s, was the first literary acknowledgement of just how nasty little girls can be. Her characters didn't josh and push as little boys are expected to do (more on this in Chapters Two and Five; I use the word 'expected' advisedly), but her characters typified the power struggles that can exist among girls and the underhand ways in which they demonstrate their cruelty. There are four friends: Grace, Elaine, Carol and Cordelia. Elaine is the victim, Cordelia the bully. Here Elaine describes their meeting at the bus stop on their way to school.

> *'Grace is waiting there and Carol and, especially, Cordelia. Once I'm outside the house there is no getting away from them. They are on the school bus, where Cordelia stands close beside me and whispers in my ear: "Stand up straight! People are looking!"*
>
> *Carol is in my classroom and it's her job to report to Cordelia what I do and say all day . . . they comment on the kind of lunch I have, how I hold my sandwich, how I chew. On the way home from school I have to walk in front of them or behind. In front is worse because they talk about how I'm walking, how I look from behind . .*
>
> *But Cordelia doesn't do these things or have this power over me because she's my enemy. Far from it. I know about enemies. There are enemies in the schoolyard, they yell things at each other and if they are boys they fight. With enemies you feel hatred, and anger. But Cordelia is my friend. She likes me. She wants to help me, they all do. They are my friends, my girlfriends. My best friends. I have never had any before and I'm terrified of losing them. I want to please.'*

Cordelia's torture goes on for many months and culminates in Elaine's life being put at risk by her so-called friends. Cordelia doesn't like the hat Elaine's wearing, takes it from her head and throws it over a bridge onto frozen water (the novel is set in Canada). Elaine is forced to go and fetch it, gets into trouble on the ice and expects the girls will be waiting to rescue her. They haven't. They've simply walked away. Not necessarily such sugar and spice, then.

Nevertheless, the fiction that girls are good and boys are bad persists. In the same *Sunday Times* article in which Davies and Clark appeared (see page 9) the respected psychologist at University College London, Dorothy Einon, seemed to perpetuate the myth.

> '*Many of the reasons why girls used to be unacceptable in society no longer exist. In addition they are not usually going to be involved in crime or violence, they are much less likely to die from an accident or illness and the potential for heartbreak is much less these days. Economic and social attitudes have been transformed. Girls no longer have to be married off at great expense. Parents are no longer worried about their reputations being besmirched by unmarried daughters becoming pregnant.*'

No acknowledgement that girls are capable of violence, and do, increasingly, as their movements become less restricted than in the past, get involved in crime, and that class and poverty are as likely to influence behaviour patterns and aspirations as is gender.

Then the Dads began to pitch in. Martin Amis, Nicholas Coleridge and Peter Kingston all wrote about how fathers were going 'Girl Crazy' and valuing their daughters where in other times they might have cheered only the arrival of a son. Girls, they claimed, ARE sugar and spice and all things nice. Cleaner, cleverer, less likely to knock over the Ming vases and faithfully Daddy's girl to the end. At the time I wrote a newspaper article, which, yet again, was my infuriated response to such gender stereotyping.

> '*How useful it will be, now it's no longer quite the done thing to replace the older model in middle age with a younger spouse or*

girlfriend, to have a daughter to trot out à la Chirac, Clinton, John Major or Martin Bell. A son, says the adage is yours till he takes a wife, a girl is yours for life.

So, what shall we do with the slugs, snails and puppy dog's tails? The juvenile action men, exam failures, university dropouts, car jackers and grunts? The guided missiles set to destroy sitting rooms and the social order? Suffocation is said to be effective. Starvation works well, preferably on a hillside or in an abandoned house, so you don't hear the pitiful cries. Poisonous oleander daubed on the tongue is quicker and apparently painless. There's abortion, or, with high-tech reproductive methods, you need never conceive a male.

None of this is journalistic fantasy from the satirical school of Jonathon Swift. It's the fate of many millions of baby girls and female foetuses. In the late '90s, the journal Theory and Time, published in North East China, wrote of a small district of Shenyang Province, "Every year, no fewer than twenty abandoned baby girls are found in dustbins or corners." Ultrasound scanners were described as "an accomplice in throttling the life of the female foetus". UNICEF in a similar report stated, "There is perhaps no more shameful statistic than the fact that some forty to fifty million girls and women are missing from the Indian population." But, I hear you cry, not in this country, not in the civilised West! I refer you to a recent article in the Express newspaper, "Doctor who will advise on aborting girl babies", the doctor of the headline operates in Cheshire. The News of the World pointed to three doctors, all in London, who would offer the same "service".

What dangerous territory we enter when we place more value on one gender than the other. The women's movement, except at its most outrageous and ridiculous, never intended the promotion of girls' interests at the expense of boys'. Equal opportunity means encouragement for all, so how can we now claim to dote on our daughters and denigrate our sons? How can we expect these down-trodden lads to become the husbands and fathers our daughters and grandchildren deserve? It's surely time to cut the critique and be constructive, rather than leave our boys floundering in a sea of rhetoric about the renegotiation of relationships and the changing *nature of the workplace, believing their dads were all bad and they are even worse. They'll lash back and who could blame them?'*

I stand by every harsh word.

I must confess, though, that I personally found it difficult and confusing to even consider the idea of becoming a mother to a son. For nine months the imaginary baby I carried around was called Eve. Like so many others I was infected by the idea that boys would be noisy, rowdy, violent creatures with inherent criminal tendencies and no prospects in what was beginning to be perceived as a feminised culture. (We do so often forget how under-represented women are even today in politics and the upper echelons of industry or the professions.)

I am also the only daughter of an only daughter and blithely assumed that it would be my lot to follow an established pattern. Curiously, the fact that my father is the youngest of five sons and my partner has four older brothers never entered my antenatal imagination.

What a girl my Eve was going to be. I chose her name with what now seems an almost embarrassing degree of pointed political sensibility. She would be a kind of first woman, born brave and strong into a world where her talents would be universally recognised and nurtured. I would understand what she would need to survive as a girl and then as a woman. She'd be a mini-me, but better. Mine would be the first generation of mothers for whom the words, 'It's a girl', would not be considered a sign of breeding failure. For months I chattered to her about how we would shop for lovely clothes together, giggle over the same jokes and share a passion for Dorothy Parker and Madame Bovary. I had her called to the bar, becoming a Queen's Counsel and sitting on the highest bench in the land before she was out of nappies. I could not have been more mistaken. So much for getting to know your baby whilst still in the womb!

As Edward emerged, the words 'He's here, he's here!' burst from his wildly excited father. The midwife shrieked, 'Ooooh! It's a boy! A big strong boy!'. Their triumphalist tones suggested that I had been quite wrong to think a girl would be welcomed with the words 'big', 'brave' or 'strong'. Other parents to whom I've spoken who were present at the birth of their daughters, confirm my suspicion that the arrival of a girl no longer engenders an air of commiseration, but she is welcomed with a softer, sweeter air. 'Ah!' say the midwives, 'you've got a little girl. See how delicate and pretty she is.'

A father of two sons, Richard Denton is a freelance filmmaker and former editor of *Everyman* on BBC2. He took on the staff job when he was left alone with his small twins – a boy and a girl, Nicholas and Alexandra, now fourteen – so that he could regulate his working day around the children. He also has an older son, from an earlier marriage: Oliver is twenty-five and went to live with his mother when his parents separated. Thus, as Richard explains, he's been an absent father, albeit one who kept in close touch with his son, and a single father. He is very conscious of how gender inequality manifests itself within seconds of birth.

His reaction to the birth of Oliver was, he says 'Pretty standard. I just went around the hospital feeling sorry for anyone who hadn't had a son. Literally, the other fathers would say they'd had a girl and I would say, "Oh, I'm so sorry". Then when my second lot were born and it was a boy and a girl, everyone was delighted and reassured. My own father's response was visceral. He was thrilled and said, "The man's done the job". The women had the same excitement. It was as if I'd achieved the ideal of two sons – the heir and the spare – and a little girl as an insurance policy for my old age. And I'm quite sure that different response is immediately passed on to the children.'

It's difficult to admit that I was at first stunned with disbelief when told in those thrilled tones that I had given birth to a son, as I've never for one second wanted my boys to think that they were not everything I've ever wanted, but I did immediately demand proof, checking first, as all new mothers do, for the presence of ten intact fingers and toes and then taking a hasty, sneaky look at the extra appendage that would confirm I had been told the truth. But I was also quickly and curiously infected with that old idea that I had 'done good' to bring a boy into the world. 'My son,' I kept whispering to myself, 'MY SON!'

I don't know how fathers feel about their daughters, but my initial alarm at the gender of my new baby disappeared the moment I ceased to concentrate on his nether regions and met his eyes – blue, penetrating and knowing. He looked at me as if we'd known each other all our lives and I simply fell, hook, line and sinker. I remember the Irish novelist, Edna O'Brien telling me once in an interview in that dulcet, husky, sexy, Irish lilt of hers, that she was in love with her sons and I, honestly, at the time, thought her a bit of a pervert. Now I understand exactly what she meant and I know I couldn't have felt it about another girl. It's not a sexual feeling, heaven forfend, but it is a sensuous, absolute passion for a member of the opposite sex who represents the apotheosis of everything a woman could desire. He is, after all, that supremely self-serving combination of one's own genes and those of the man chosen as a lover and lifelong companion!

I should say that when Charlie was born four years later, I didn't suffer the shock or even a smidgen of disappointment at having another boy, partly because I already knew he was a Charles and not a Charlotte long before he was born. At the first scan I'd told the radiologist I really didn't want to know, I'd leave it till he was born, but . . . he happened to be lying with his legs spread wide apart and, as the scanner slid rapidly over the relevant bit, we couldn't help but notice that he was indisputably male. And this time I was thrilled. I'd had four fabulous years of fun, cuddles and hilarity with his older brother and all I wished for was what we should all desire – a healthy baby – male or female.

But there's no denying my unexpected delight first time around in producing a boy and when I look for its roots it comes, I think, partly from my own upbringing. For as long as I can remember my mother would remind me, in jokey terms, of course, that her fantasy baby had not been Jennifer Susan, but David Robert. I'm an only child, so a girl was all she had and I guess I subconsciously tried to fulfil what I believed were her disappointed dreams. I rejected any attempts to interest me in the domestic and was familiar on first name terms with all the doctors and nurses at our local hospital as a result of regular injuries from scraps or incidents with the gang of lads I ran with on the street.

I fell out of trees, had to be dragged from near drowning after being the only one to take the dare to walk across the ice on a filthy duck pond, came off a fantastically speedy, homemade go-kart whilst racing downhill, and grazed my knees with alarming regularity from frequent falls in our games of cowboys and Indians. My preferred outfit was a pair of scruffy dungarees, but for the Wild West I had an Annie Oakley outfit with a great fringed weskit, belt with six guns, but, rather impractically, a culottes skirt! They called me a tomboy, which I generally took as a huge compliment.

When I started to read for myself, it was George in Enid Blyton's *Famous Five* who took my fancy. Nothing soppy about her. She never made the sandwiches or remembered the pop, but climbed trees and solved crimes. How I wished my parents had called me Roberta or Charlotte, which I too could have shortened to a boy's name – Bobby or Charlie seemed so much more attractive than Jennifer, inspired by some glamorous and no doubt girlie movie star called Jennifer Jones.

I'm not sure whether or not I was born with a higher testosterone level than the average girl. I've certainly never felt I needed to be backward in pushing myself forward and have always felt my dad's role as breadwinner to be the one that best suited me rather than my mother's role as dedicated homemaker. But I do know that my behaviour was considered on the whole to be culturally acceptable, and there were available role models, such as Blyton's George or Doris Day cracking her whip on the Deadwood Stage, even in the 1950's. This is just another example of how girls were permitted to indulge their masculinity, long before the women's movement, in a way that hasn't really begun to open up for our boys.

I have to say that, whilst I'm perfectly prepared to accept (having changed my life infinitely for the better – in terms of energy and skin and hair quality – with hormone replacement therapy) that hormones do play a role in male and female wellbeing, I'm extremely reluctant to go along with the 'science' that claims our abilities and personalities are determined by whether it's oestrogen or testosterone that runs through our endocrine systems. Steve Biddulph in *Raising Boys* discusses a condition called Congenital Adrenal Hyperplasia which can 'give girls excess testosterone in the womb, but this is remedied once the child is born. Though they are hormonally normal from then on, these girls show above average athletic skills, as well as a preference for male playmates, toy cars and guns, and "masculine" clothes.' Now I scored full house on the latter, but have always been absolute rubbish at any sport or athletics.

Equally he writes, 'An excess sensitivity to testosterone or an excess of it, has been linked to mathematical ability, left-handedness and a very high incidence of asthma and allergies.' I have asthma, can't walk into a house that has a cat in it without my eyes streaming and airways blocking, am right-handed and so bad at maths they wouldn't let me take it at 'O' level. I haven't even developed the talent whereby all journalists bump up their income – learning how to make a great work of fiction out of an expenses claim. So, I'm afraid I take all these hormonal classifications with a huge pinch of salt.

My mother has always underplayed the David Robert business and my father has regularly declared himself delighted to have a daughter, but an interesting and enlightening incident occurred soon after Edward's birth. We hadn't been home from hospital for more than a couple of hours, a mere twenty-four hours after his birth, and the new little family was curled up in bed getting to know itself. We heard the back door open, followed by rapid, anxious footsteps crossing the hall and rushing post haste up the stairs. The bedroom door swung open and my mother flew in, scurried around to my side of the bed, wrenched my baby from my arms, held him aloft and uttered words that remain emblazoned on my brain, 'At last my boy!'

Four little words which, at the age of thirty-three and with half a lifetime of achievement behind me, swept away all her attempts to convince me that I had been 'good enough'. It was not a good start to our new relationship as mother and grandmother; I snatched Edward back from her clutches and found myself unable to resist my response, 'Actually, mother, he's MY boy, not yours.' We have talked about it since and I know she loves me dearly. We've even become closer as we've grown older, sharing the worries and anxieties that come with the territory of being a mother, but I doubt

I'll ever quite set aside that muddling sense of sadness at never feeling quite enough for her, or the pride felt in achieving what she hadn't. What dangerous territory we enter, as I've said, when we appear to value one gender over another.

Other women I've talked to have admitted to this same irrational delight after the production of a son – which would seem to indicate that even the most fervently feminist among us have yet to shake off the conditioning of two thousand years of male supremacy! For Lynne Segal, Annual Professor of Psychology and Gender at Birkbeck College, London University, the birth of her boy Zim in 1969 came '. . . before I had any awareness of feminism as a movement. I was accidentally pregnant and the only thing I knew for sure was that I didn't want a child, male or female. But I was then completely implanted with the views of the time, having imbibed the idea of female inferiority with my mother's milk, my father's endless derision of all things feminine and the seamless cultural consensus on this. "Better luck next time," he'd say unfailingly to his patients giving birth to daughters. He hardly ever spoke to his own. I was therefore most relieved to have a son, in the sense of regarding it as less of a total catastrophe than if I had had a daughter. So that inner sense of female insignificance existed so strongly in me (which I believe we never lose once it has been so firmly implanted in childhood).'

The columnist and novelist, India Knight, has two boys, Oscar who's ten and Archie who's seven, both born as the fashion was beginning to shift from boys to girls, and India, as a leading cultural commentator, was well aware of the zeitgeist. Nevertheless she felt, 'Absolute delight obviously; also a slightly guilt-inducing un-PC sense of having done marvellously by producing males (especially the first time). Given that one isn't Ann Boleyn, this is an absurd sort of reaction, but there you go – I still had it. I felt extremely pleased with myself, especially since the women in my family tend to have girls. My granny was one of seven, I myself have two sisters.

Also, it somehow felt extra miraculous: I could just about see how I might be able to produce a girly mini-me by some sort of weird internal cloning process, but producing a great big BOY seemed extraordinarily ingenious and clever. Do you know that line from Macbeth where he says to her, "Bring forth men children only/for your undaunted mettle should compose/nothing but males"? It often pops into my head, quite madly and paranoically, when I ask myself why I have no daughters.'

Diane Abbott, the labour MP for Hackney, now forty-nine has James who's eleven. She knew before James was born that she was having a son and felt, as I did, that

'tiny, infinitesimal disappointment, partly, I think, born out of narcissism that I would have preferred a mini-me. But it's also because I know how to survive as a black woman and I worried about the fact I would have to raise a black boy, which adds an extra dimension of concern. Society is very threatened by black men and because my marriage was shaky at the time I knew I was probably going to have to do this job by myself. So there were the trivial worries – what do you do with a mysterious creature that leaves the toilet seat up and plays ball – stereotypes, I know, but much more seriously how could I encourage him to be his own person? Let him be powerful and at the same time protect him from a society that will see a physically boisterous black boy as a threat?'

The least ambiguous and most guilt-free parents I spoke to during the research for this book were Jenny and Martin Stephen. She's head teacher of a mixed secondary school in Cheshire and her husband, Martin, is High Master of the Manchester Grammar School, so they both have a lifetime of experience of teaching both girls and boys. Martin has also worked in facilities for youthful offenders and is consequently familiar with the opposite extremes of young male behaviour – the very bright, well supported and motivated and the ones who, for whatever reason, have gone off the rails.

Unusually for people who have risen so high in the teaching profession their careers have run in parallel, although Jenny did work part-time whilst each baby was very small and then went back permanently full-time when the third son was six. The three of them are now all adult. Neil is twenty-six, Simon twenty-four and Henry twenty-one. Martin will confess to the fact that he would have liked just one girl, although in the end he realised he was simply relieved that his babies were well and concerned that they should grow up to be fully rounded human beings, regardless of their gender, but Jenny is adamant that she was delighted with her lot.

'I was absolutely thrilled and never gave a thought to whether or not I would have preferred a girl. In fact, I think through the three pregnancies, we only ever discussed one girl's name and that was because Martin suggested we might think about it. I think it was because for five years I had taught only boys and I absolutely adored them. I found them attentive, kind, energetic, very individual, but at the same time extremely robust and fun to be with. I always knew where I stood with the boys, whereas girls can be a little more underhand!'

I've been thrilled to find so many parents, even in today's apparent anti-boy climate who are so ready to share their absolute joy in their sons, although I do think we need to exercise some caution in the manner in which we greet and treat them. We're probably never going to stop fathers, midwives or even ourselves – as the cultural delight in boys seems so inbred – from greeting our sons with such an excess of bold enthusiasm; but I do think we need to think carefully about the pressure we might be subtly imposing upon them to be a particular kind of male – strong and literally fighting fit – from the moment of birth.

It's just not fair to put them into a box marked macho at such an early stage, no matter how flattering it might be to the female ego to consider herself a latter day Lady Macbeth with the mettle to bring forth only males, or for a father to see immediately the meaty legs and powerful shoulders that will take his little one to lead England onto the pitch at Twickenham to a triumph in the Five Nations (something he never achieved no matter how hard he tried, but for which his son might have neither the talent nor the inclination). Try saying 'how sweet' in a soft voice to a new-born baby boy and watch him purr with pleasure!

It's generally nowadays not left to mothers to take sole physical care of their sons. Long gone are the days when it was acceptable for a man to say in public, as the DIY expert, Barry Bucknell said on *Woman's Hour* in the late '40s, 'I do like to spend some time with my children, perhaps even help with the bath before bedtime, but NAPPIES, now that's another matter. I don't mind whipping off a wet one and popping on a dry one, but if it's anything more than that . . . definitely not.' And I guess he was quite advanced for his day. My partner, David, loved being closely physically involved with both our sons and it was often a battle over who would do the bath or change the nappy because we all, he, I, and the fantastic nanny, Jeanne, who stayed with us for six wonderful years, enjoyed being close to their little, soft, wriggly bodies. David, who was a naval officer at the time, even has the distinction of being the only sailor to have changed a nappy on board a nuclear submarine during a Family Day visit, and berated the shipmates who found his behaviour a little unmanly.

But women are frequently still the primary carers for their baby boys and it's a daunting prospect, as India Knight recalls: 'Initially, complete bewilderment: I didn't know what to do with Oscar's PARTS. Although I was, obviously familiar with male genitals, I'd never had a really close look (you don't really, do you, just for the loveliness of it?) until my baby was born. And I am quite girly, in some fairly full-on senses and I did briefly wonder whether raising the children in a pink house, with no man – at the time – and heavy female involvement from me, our au pair and all my female relatives, would automatically turn my sons into raging nancies. It seems to be OK!'

Linda Bellingham, the actor and former OXO Mum, also has two sons, Michael who's nineteen and a half and Rob who's nearly fifteen. The boys' father, Nuncio, is Italian, so there was no cultural ambiguity about whether it was better to have a boy or a girl.

'Thank God,' she says, 'I had boys. In Italy men still rule the roost, so I was very much approved of as a Mamma of sons. The family did find it peculiar that I had a regime for them, but from being tiny I insisted they should go to bed at six. Italians let even tiny babies stay up till all hours and then wonder why when they're toddlers

they run around, completely exhausted and are a pain in the neck. Mine, thank God, were generally admirably well behaved because they weren't knackered all the time.

What I did find difficult was Nuncio's fixed ideas and old wives tales about how to care for his son's precious parts. He was always watchful that I should wash their bits properly, but taking great care not to pull back the foreskin, in case I made it bleed. Very nerve wracking and I'm still neurotic about it, although you can't say to your nineteen-year-old, "Have you washed your penis properly?" can you? The other thing that astonished me was the way I'd lay them on their changing mat and up would stand this little organ and pee in my eye. Oh, my God! Every time!'

Now, none of us wishes to embarrass our boys, but I've heard this anxiety repeated over and over again. So, if you're new at this business, fret not. Some boys from birth have a foreskin that retracts immediately without any trouble at all (not of concern to you, of course, if you're Jewish or Muslim and the boy has been circumcised for religious reasons). Sometimes you'll notice when you're washing him, even with a small baby whose foreskin has been adhered to the penis, that it has naturally come unstuck. Usually by three or four it has retracted in most boys. Often they've done it all alone by pulling and playing with themselves: nothing to worry about, it's comforting and fun and they know when to stop if it hurts – you don't. It is important, once the foreskin has retracted, to encourage regular washing to keep everything clean and infection free.

In very rare cases it can take years for the foreskin to retract, but in a special programme broadcast on Radio 4 in 1998 about circumcision carried out in the '60s and '70s for 'medical' reasons on boys of eight or ten, a specialist in genito-urinary medicine said that, left alone, a foreskin would always retract naturally, sometimes as late as teenage, and should not be a matter of concern for children or parents.

According to Professor Jeffrey Weeks, the author of *Sex, Politics and Society*, the fashion for circumcising boys among the English upper and middle classes began in the 1890s and became almost a mania, as concerns about the sexuality of adolescent boys grew in the Victorian era:

> 'Dr Remondino attacked the "debatable appendage" in his History of Circumcision (1891), and compared circumcision to a "well secured life annuity", "a better saving investment", making for a greater capacity for labour, a longer life, less nervousness, fewer doctors' bills. By the 1930s at least two thirds of all public school boys were circumcised (compared to only one-tenth of working-class boys) and by then perhaps one third of the male population was circumcised, with very little medical justification.'

Those men who spoke on the radio, by the way, talked very movingly about how frightened and anxious they had been when they were taken into hospital, how painful the whole process had been and how much in later life they felt they had been mutilated. This doesn't seem to be the case among men who have the operation as babies as part of a religious tradition, presumably because they are not made to feel different from the men who are closest to them, but it is obviously a step that needs to be considered very carefully and perhaps avoided in any other circumstance.

As far as testicles are concerned, generally both will be visible by the time the baby is checked at six weeks by the health visitor. If not, they need to be monitored. Only one mum of my wide acquaintance of parents found that her boy had a problem with an undescended testicle and it was fixed with a simple operation when he was in his early teens.

As far as peeing in your face goes, and Linda Bellingham is not the only one to have had this unpleasant experience, it's hard at first to convince yourself, especially as a particularly cheeky look seems to come over your son when he does it, that this is not his first mini act of defiance. It does, however, seem to be a wholly involuntary action, probably created by some excess testosterone, left over from the pregnancy. It's the testosterone, apparently, which brings about a baby boy's erections and when he wees without his nappy on, as you are leaning over him to clean him up or tickle his tummy, it happens to be pointing right at you. Just bad luck, I'm afraid.

I've discussed some of my thinking on the nature/nurture debate already – and there'll be more on the subject in the next chapter. Whilst I do believe that we at times overplay the difference between boys and girls and men and women when we should be encouraging and celebrating the whole range of different types of girls and boys, it would be foolish to dismiss the existence of testosterone and its influence on a boy's development at different stages in his life – as a foetus when his sex organs are growing, as a small baby, at around six when he begins to look physically more boyish, and during puberty when he's turning from boy into man.

There's also some evidence that levels of testosterone are linked to the conditions in which a boy lives. One study found that boys who are raised in a violent or aggressive environment had higher testosterone levels than those where the ethos of their surroundings was gentler and more supportive. Kate Adie, the BBC's chief correspondent, says she has observed this phenomenon in battle, which she describes as 'a kind of testosterone-fuelled madness'.

What no-one has tested, of course, is whether there are raised levels of testosterone, too, in environments where women have been forced to join battle – as in Russia at the end of the Second World War when women joined up for the front line, preferring to defend themselves on the battlefield than be raped or murdered in their homes. It's important, I think, that as mothers we remember we have testosterone, too; it may play a part in violence and aggression in both sexes, but its effects can be ameliorated by a kind, loving and supportive upbringing. As Katherine Hepburn said to Humphrey Bogart in *The African Queen*, 'Human nature, Mr Allnut, is what we were put on this earth to rise above.'

Whatever the facts, and the jury is still out on the science, it doesn't help to make snide and sexist remarks (although I've done so myself and shouldn't have) about testosterone pinging off the walls and being an altogether bad thing. Nor am I happy with the frequently expressed opposite theories, which seem to suggest testosterone is an altogether wonderful substance, making for great leadership qualities or determining a boy's sporting prowess. How confusing to be told, on the one hand, that your naturally occurring hormone makes you violent and aggressive and, on the other, that it defines your masculinity and will make you more successful. It's terribly sad for those boys who really don't want to be Prime Minister or Captain of the England football team. Boys need reassurance about their nature – whatever it may be. They certainly don't need to be told either that their make-up gives them natural advantages and superiority, or that it consigns them to a future as an angry young man.

I've never, as I've said, wanted my sons to think they were somehow second best, but I can't deny that there were moments in the first months and years of my children's lives when I wondered how on earth I would cope with being the only female in an all male household (working on *Woman's Hour* has been a wonderful antidote!). How would I learn to kick or throw a ball, would I ever master the art of putting Lego and Meccano together and would I ever see the fascination, which seems to infect all small boys at some time, of a tractor or a digger?

I remember visiting a friend's house soon after Ed's birth and a few days before her wedding to a divorcee whose teenage son had come over from America for the wedding. As he curled his enormous frame around her sofa, grunted his responses to our questions, hauled himself up onto enormous size 13 trainers and tottered around the tiny flat with the co-ordination of a blind armadillo, my heart sank as I envisaged my perfect tiny baby developing into such a creature. I expressed these concerns to another now ex-friend, who hovered at the time around the more extreme edges of the radical feminist movement. 'Poor you,' she muttered, 'having to raise one of the enemy. Boys will be boys!' 'Not necessarily,' I replied and crossed her off my Christmas card list.

Chapter Two

Boys will be boys

'Boys will be boys.' How many times have I heard that expression from grannies, aunties, even friends, who really should know better, when the boys have done something particularly violent, stupid or dangerous? He's fallen over because he was running too fast without looking where he was going and needs half a dozen stitches in his chin. 'Ah well, boys will be boys!' He's whacked someone over the head with a baseball bat at playschool. 'Ah well, boys will be boys.' He's come off a bend in the rain in fourth gear at forty miles an hour a mere month after passing his test, even though he's been told a million times to change down, take it slowly and be extra careful in wet weather conditions. 'Ah well, boys will be boys.' They are, I've concluded, the most dangerous words in the English language.

And what precisely do they mean? That traditionally we have expected our boys to behave badly or stupidly or irresponsibly, and looked on indulgently and made excuses for them when they do. Boys are dim, boys are rough, boys are emotionally illiterate, but hey, that's OK because boys will be boys! Thus, whilst girls are told they can be anything they want to be, flattered into believing that they are not only clever, but kind, communicative and hard-working, and are constantly reassured that every assistance will be forthcoming to enable them to achieve their goals, boys see raised eyebrows everywhere and hear that expression which suggests they are irredeemable, but, hell, we love them anyway.

No wonder they have a reputation for running about like head-less chickens, leaving a trail of dirty shoes and socks, joshing and smashing into each other with the concentration span of a flea. Let's consider for a moment that this has nothing whatsoever to do with the testosterone running through their veins, but something to do with being given permission. You may think you're saying no, no, boys, pipe down, don't run around so much, but what they are actually hearing is, 'She doesn't mean it, she really thinks boys will be boys and she really doesn't mind.' Boys will be boys is an expression, which should be banned. It certainly is in my house.

Next time you're at playschool, nursery, infant school or even at a friend's house where there are boys and girls, watch out for the subtle 'It's a Boy' and 'Ah, sweet little thing' messages that continue long after they're no longer babes in arms. Watch the small boy who goes to fiddle with the television channel changer (clicker flicker as we call it, after Charlie's propensity to flick and click when he was younger – and still does if he's allowed to get away with it) and observe the indulgent smiles on the faces of the adults. 'There he goes, he's so interested in technology,' they sigh. Now notice the way a girl is told, 'Give that to Mummy sweetheart, you don't want to be messing about with that, you might break it.'

If she's about to leap off the same wall as her brother, you can bet your bottom dollar he'll have been told how brave he is, she'll have been warned not to hurt herself and to come in and sit down quietly (knees together!). You'll see this difference in every aspect of their lives whether it's running, jumping, playing with dolls, cars, tractors, Lego, helping with the dusting. Subtle little hints that some things are all right for boys to do and some are OK for girls.

So, when Kevin, a colleague at work, tells me he's pretty convinced that girls and boys really are different he cites the example of his two-and-a-half-year-old son, Will. When Will first started going to playgroup, he made a beeline for the little pram and spent hours pushing it around. So they bought him his own pram and a 'baby' to go in it. Will loved his dolly. He gave him a boy's name, Dom, laid him on a blanket and pretended to change his nappy, cuddled and kissed him. Will played with Dom for hours.

Then, one day, around the age of two he simply stopped playing with his dolly. Poor Dom was left in a corner and forgotten about. Will did start pushing the pram again, but this time Dom was replaced by a tractor. When Kevin reflects on what brought about the sudden change, he remembers that it coincided with a new best friend: 'a very boysie boy who was totally into cars and football, so Will went along with him.' Kevin concedes that, had it not been for the influence of the other boy and the implication that dolls were not suitable toys for a boy, Will might have continued to enjoy both Dom and the tractors.

Kevin does, reluctantly, confess to having been slightly relieved when the doll period passed – he remembers funny looks in the park in St Albans. I wouldn't argue for forcing a boy to play with dolls, but it seems a pity that he's not reassured by everyone around him (family, teachers and strangers) that a boy who likes to act out looking after a baby can also find a digger or a tractor absolutely thrilling – without being thought bizarre.

Let me describe some children and see if you can guess their gender from their interests and inclinations. Pair number one, both from the same family.

1 A

1. Liked dolls as a small child.
2. Loves clothes.
3. Not very academic.
4. Does ballet, wants to be a professional dancer.

B

1. Always liked to kick a ball around as a child.
2. Not too bothered about clothes.
3. Very academic.
4. Played football for Manchester City Juniors and now hockey for the county.

And pair number two, also from the same family.

2 A

1. Loves animals.

2. Hates football and rugby.
3. Likes to ride horses.
4. Detests shopping, especially for clothes.
5. Loves to cook.
6. Brilliant at maths and science.
7. Loathes reading fiction (proudly boasts a B in English Literature at GCSE without ever having read the set texts!).
8. Great talker, especially about feelings, relationships, plans.
9. Cuts own hair at home.
10. Despises all scents and perfumes.

B

1. Dislikes all cats and dogs.
2. Loves playing rugby and watching football.
3. Nervous around horses.
4. Loves to shop especially for clothes.
5. Cooks when it's absolutely necessary.
6. Leans towards languages, history and philosophy.
7. Likes reading fiction.
8. Sometimes open about feelings, sometimes grunty.
9. Revels in a session at the hairdressers.
10. Has an impressive array of scents and skin care products.

In the first family, A is a boy – Richard Denton's fourteen-year-old son, Nicholas, twin to child B, his sister Alexandra. And the second family is mine own. A is Ed and B is Charlie – both boys. It's a small illustration, but it does show that if boys are raised with an open mind and not pressed into assumptions about their gender, they don't necessarily get stuck in the stereotypes expected of them. Nevertheless it is a constant battle for parents to protect them from a culture that has certain expectations of boys and seems increasingly to put them down whichever way they jump. 'Poofs' if they like to dance, rugger buggers if they're into more 'manly' pursuits.

Kate Kellaway is the mother of four sons of her own and two stepsons. Like me she became angry at the underlying assumption that all boys are hopeless cases, stuck in some macho, power-crazed, football-fuelled fantasy land. She wrote in the *Observer* in the late '90s in response to Allison Pearson's article in which she had described girls as 'hot, girls are desirable, girls are the future, girls are the new boys'. Kate commented:

'When I tell people I have six boys, the reflex response is "Almost a football team!" At first I used to agree with the groan that almost seemed to be called for. But now I've started a line in mild dissent. Some of the boys are good at football, others are not. Each boy is different.

It has become permissible to be sexist about boys in a way that would be unthinkable if it were girls you were talking about. (A family with six daughters would never attract the comment "A sewing circle!".) If I have learnt anything through having boys, it is that identity is more than gender.

To know that you have a boy or girl is only the beginning of knowledge. And yet boyism (to coin a phrase) is rife and it's awful to think that it could distort a mother's expectation of her son. When my youngest son was born, as soon as he had the nerve to open his mouth and cry, the midwife observed as she stared into his puce, crushed face, that he was a "typical little man". He was not. He was a crying baby. If he had been a girl, she would have comforted him.'

This last story is a very familiar one to me. When Ed was only a few days old, the midwife or health visitor, I don't remember which, came round to check him over and take a blood test from his heel. She warned me that it would be just a little prick, but that he'd probably scream the place down. I waited in terrified anticipation, dreading the moment when my perfect little boy would first have to endure pain – there's something about being a new mum that makes you hypersensitive to all forms of torture.

I remember once sitting weeping uncontrollably on the bathroom floor as he kicked happily without his nappy. I'd taken those few moments where he was amusing himself to read the newspaper and was heartbroken about an Amnesty International report on men and women in Chile who had been broken down by the authorities by being forced to witness their children's torture. It's ridiculous to compare such horrors with a simple medical procedure, but I still felt terror at the thought that he might be hurt.

She stuck the needle in him whilst I held him and he didn't even whimper. He just looked at me with absolute disdain and shock, seemingly wondering why on earth I, who was supposed to protect him, was allowing someone to cause him pain. He didn't cry at all, eliciting from the silly health professional the comment, 'There you are, you see, he took it like a man.' No, he didn't. He took it like a baby betrayed.

Kate, in her article, goes on,

> 'Boys are hard work, but hard work is rewarding. Of course, it is true that some boys fight all the time. I have a friend who gave her son a Barbie doll. With a swift flick of her hip, he converted Barbie into a gun. But when I gave my twins (aged two and a half) baby dolls after the birth of my last son, one of them was wonderful to his baby, the other was downright cavalier. He looked at me blankly when I presented him with the doll. Their reactions to the baby are in keeping with this. One of them rushes to wipe milk from the baby's chin, the other takes little notice of his brother (except to put lush maroon lipstick on his mouth).
>
> What is seldom recorded is that boys can be loving, conversational, witty and even (sometimes) quiet. And with boys you know it is the real thing. Boys don't cravenly try to please; they aren't, as some girls are, approval seeking hostesses by the time they are five.'

So how do we, as parents, help boys negotiate the minefield of expectations and derisions that they may have to face in the outside world from the moment they're born, and encourage them to develop into the men they want to be? In the early years it's generally easier because, if they are cared for at home or in an enlightened environment where they are defined as children, rather than as boys or girls, the pressures they face to conform to an ideal should be minimal, although, even as switched-on parents, we have to be wary of the 'boys will be boys' syndrome and of our own ingrained prejudices. I once heard myself, to my horror, saying,

'You naughty boy, just wait till your father gets home.' Portraying Dad as a disciplinarian ogre was not helpful to man or boy.

As Angela Phillips points out in her book *The Trouble With Boys* we have to be very careful with what we say directly to our boys or in their hearing, perhaps when chatting to our friends. On the one hand there is still a dangerous tendency, as we saw in Chapter One, to be over-enthusiastic about the arrival of a boy, rather than a girl and to give a boy a sense of his own superiority. What is more common nowadays, but equally insidious, is the tendency to complain about the men in our lives. Phillips writes:

> *'Disappointment breeds resentment and those men who castigate feminists for breeding man hatred would be appalled by the level of antipathy towards men expressed by very ordinary women who have never been touched by ideas about separatism and would never classify themselves as feminists, women for whom contemptuous grumbling about male incompetence is only matched by their fear of the strangers who stalk the street, grab innocent children and wreak vengeance on women through violent sex.*
>
> *These mothers may well see their sons as exempt from this condemnation of the male world, but it will be harder for their sons to exempt themselves. A boy who grows up being told men are bad can choose either to be bad as well, to side with his mother and despise himself or to reject his mother and everything she stands for.'*

So, tempting as it may be to grumble that he 'doesn't put the toothpaste top on in the morning, never changes the loo roll, can't find his way to the washing machine and has gone to the pub, again . . .', it's not a good idea to make even the most minor dissatisfactions apparent to our boys. It's not their problem if our marriages or partnerships are beset by irritations and it doesn't help them to feel that their dads – their closest models for what it means to be male – are somehow substandard people. (Naturally this is helped enormously when dads pull their weight on the domestic front, and does not apply if the father is violent – see more in Chapters Five and Seven.)

Richard Denton is convinced that his twins are happily following their own interests, sometimes contrary to their assumed gender roles, because he made a conscious decision when they were small never to treat them differently and never to insist that the boy did 'guy' stuff and vice versa for the girl. Around the time the children were born he was making a film with Dr Jonathon Miller who was very interested in some research, which was carried out in America in the '40s and '50s.

A group of women, given babies to look after and play with, were filmed for the experiment. What the women didn't realise was that they were given the same baby twice and told, on the first occasion, that it was a boy, and on the second occasion that it was girl. (Obviously the women were not asked to bathe or change the babies!) Richard watched the resulting film and says he was astonished to see how differently the women reacted, depending on what gender they assumed the infant to be. If the 'boy' cried, he was jollied along and told big boys didn't do that. If the 'girl' cried, she was comforted, hugged and kissed.

As the parent at home from when the twins were toddlers, Richard was closely involved in their upbringing. He decided to treat them both exactly the same. Play was often pretty physical and if he swung one around, he would swing the other. Both responded well. If either cried or was upset he was sympathetic and cuddly. The result, he says, is that their gender roles have not been reversed, but broadened:

> *'In many ways, she is the tough and physical one and he is sensitive and gentle, but it's not a hard and fast rule. He really did like playing with dolls when he was small and she wasn't too fussed, much preferring to kick a ball around.*
>
> *They both went to ballet when they were about four. Their mother had taken them to see The Nutcracker and they really enjoyed it – so they went off to a ballet class just down the road. And that's where his physical abilities came out. He loved it and she wasn't at all keen. He will I'm sure become a professional dancer – he's very talented. She's pretty physical too and played for Manchester City for a bit and then decided she preferred hockey.*

She plays for the County and it could be that she saw hockey as a game in which girls are more generally accepted than football and she'll be able to take it further and be taken seriously. That hasn't really happened in football yet.'

On two occasions we went through with Edward the difficulties of trying to support him in an interest, which was not seen as masculine. When he was three we took him to see the musical *42nd Street*, which has a lot of noisy and energetic tap dancing. Both the men and women were fit, strong and powerful. We sat in the fourth row from the front, with Edward on the edge of his seat throughout. As the company prepared to do the big title number his little voice piped up in a stage whisper audible to the entire theatre, 'I wish I was up there with them.'

He'd like to try it, he announced, after the theatre. So, like Richard, we found a little local dancing class and Edward went every week. It was a bit Billy Elliott – he was the only boy in the class, but the girls didn't tease or make fun of him. They just accepted him. He asked for special shoes from Father Christmas and got them, despite my Dad's reservations (not voiced to Edward, just to me) and whilst Ed was anxious to get on with the tapping he happily went through the basic ballet training, coming home and proudly showing us the new positions he'd learned and how he could 'make a window' with his knees – the first steps to mastering 'turning out'. He loved it.

Then he started school and one Friday afternoon, when I picked him up, he got in the car, picked up the ballet bag from the seat by his side and threw it onto the floor. He looked completely miserable. 'What's the matter?' I asked him. 'I'm not going dancing anymore,' he sobbed. Some bright spark had asked him what he was doing after school. He'd said, with all the cheery innocence of a toddler, that he was going to his ballet class, the other lad called him a 'gay boy', still infuriatingly the favourite choice of insult among boys of all classes and races, and so he was giving ballet up.

You try to reassure them that liking dancing is fine for boys and girls and the person who's been rude is just stupid and ignorant (three or four is a little early to be going into the finer details of what it means to be gay, although I've always tried with both my children to introduce them to people of all races and sexual orientation so that when these terrible moments of racism, sexism or homophobia come up, as inevitably they do, I can always say, well . . . so and so is black, lives with a man, lives with a woman – whatever applies to the current topic of discussion – and they're our friend and we like them. So those people saying nasty things are just wrong.) But, of course, the peer pressure is powerful. Ed decided dancing wasn't worth sticking his neck out for, so he packed it in and tried to like football instead.

I would never have tried to force or even persuade him to continue. It's tough enough surviving out there without any pressure from parents who're trying to impose their own political point of view in terms of gender roles. By all means, talk about it at home, sympathise with the difficulties of making these hard choices, make them aware that there is an argument to be had about gender stereotyping and that things are beginning to change. Stand by them if the choice to hang in there is theirs, but don't force them into a position where they are at risk of being bullied because you're trying to create a more equitable world.

It is definitely worth making even small children aware of some of the discussions that go on about equality between men and women. It's obviously something that's talked about often in my house and even when Ed was tiny he was interested and thoughtful about what it means to be a boy and what it means to be a girl. He came home from playschool one day in high dudgeon because he'd been playing in the Home Corner, cooking and serving up an imaginary lunch (something he now likes to do for real) only to be advised by one of the play leaders that he really ought to be playing with the cars or the climbing frame.

He reported back that he'd told her without hesitation that he liked the cars and the climbing frame, but, just at that moment, he was cooking lunch and later he'd be doing the ironing, just like his daddy did (it's true, I'm a very lucky woman). He also said that his favourite toy at home at the moment was a tea set, although he did have a police motorbike as well, so after playschool he'd be dishing up tea to his teddies and his mummy when she came home from work. Then they'd be taking his bike out on the common. That shut her up, apparently.

On another occasion Ed had me bursting with pride when we went to buy new school shoes. Some of you might remember Clarks advertising a new line in footwear called Princess Shoes. They were pink or red, had a 'diamond' on the toe and a key to a 'magic kingdom' in the slightly raised heel. They were heavily promoted on television and Ed was completely seduced. The ads were rather gothic in tone and showed an Alice-In-Wonderland-type character climbing mountains and fording rivers in her new shoes, and Ed, at the age of four or five, didn't seem to notice her gender, just the 'magic' properties of the footwear.

The same middle-aged, rather conventional sales assistant in a grey suit who'd been serving us and carefully measuring Ed's feet since his first pair of shoes, greeted us and asked what we were after today. Looking past the trainers and sensible school shoes, Ed pointed to the Princess variety, 'I'd like a pair of those in my size please.' 'But,' the assistant was choking with horror, 'those are girls' shoes!' And my little chap took him on.

'If I was a girl,' he said, 'and I came in here in a pair of trousers and demanded some trainers you wouldn't say they were boys' shoes, would you? Or think I ought to be wearing a skirt? So, it's not fair. In fact,' and he looked up at me as he delivered the killer blow, 'it's sexist!' I was so bowled over by his indignation, and so impressed by the articulate construction of his argument (so much for boys not being able to string two words together!), that I bought him the shoes. It was not easy – even for someone as determined as I to give my boys every opportunity to express their masculine and feminine sides – to watch my strapping little lad mincing across Clapham Common in what were, frankly, undeniably intended as shoes for girls.

Even at that age, we women and girls seem to be pressed into a form of foot binding that is not conducive to running, jumping, climbing mountains or fording rivers and Ed soon conceded his Princess shoes were not a good idea. 'They're just not comfy, Mum,' he told me. We went back to the shop and, much to the man's relief, bought a pair of trainers. It was a costly experiment, but worth it to see the triumph on Ed's face when I bought the shoes and he won his first argument.

India Knight's two boys have so far never been pigeon-holed at school based on expectations of what boys are supposed to be like, the result, she thinks of the school being a very sweet, progressive establishment. In fact, she says, her boys have pigeon-holed themselves by being ridiculously laddish. Except when it comes to dressing up and choosing clothes.

> 'Archie's favourite colour is still pink and his favourite trainers when he was five were girls' – white with glittery purple stripes, much to the disgust of eight-year-old Oscar who just couldn't get over the gender treachery. I remember watching Archie gazing down at his feet a lot, beaming with adoration. They've never dressed up as anything particularly feminine, like my clothes, but even if they did, surely that's the point of dressing up. I don't think it would worry me. There was a child at their last school who wore women's necklaces every day and came in for a certain amount of ridicule.
>
> As for clothes that they choose – sportswear really – Oscar has fairly determined opinions, Archie is much more malleable. I buy their clothes with them, so we're all happy. They can wear anything they like as far as I'm concerned (with the possible exception of mini-suits, mini-ties and mini-grey slip ons!)'

Again it seems to me there's a delicate balance to be achieved between allowing boys to express what's just a bit of fun or even an experiment – trying on jewellery, painting nails, putting on lipstick and dressing up as a 'lady' – if they feel they want to, and putting them in a position where they are exposed to ridicule and bullying. It's certainly not a good idea to make a boy feel ashamed or odd if he wants to play around with a bit of gender bending, and, if he feels he's happy to go out to school in pink, then why not? (Remember the Victorians used pink for boys and blue for girls, so these fashions and differentiations are entirely arbitrary. Dads who are not ashamed to be seen around the kitchen in a pinny are a big help!)

It's a question, as with everything, of talking to your boys about it, perhaps engaging them in discussion about the history of costume and use of colour, thumbing through books that show what peacocks men have been at certain times in the past, and looking in contemporary magazines at some of the androgynous fashions that are around these days. Then, if they feel strongly enough about wearing a necklace to school and want to put those arguments to their friends, let them. If, on the other hand, they're worried or anxious about what reactions they might face at school or if there's any hint that they are being bullied, back them up in their decision to leave the pink trainers at home.

Diane Abbott remembers the day when her son James was forced by peer pressure to abandon his cute little Osh Kosh dungarees and sweet, soft shoes. It was when he moved from the small nursery he'd attended since he was two (and where he'd worked and played collaboratively and politely) to a big inner London primary school, which she describes as 'very big, rough, tough and shambolic'.

> *'He came into this school where the playground was like World War Three and it was obvious that only the strong survive. The first morning on the way in he was his usual sweet self, my little boy with whom I'd had an almost symbiotic relationship – an extension of myself; the second day, he got off the bus at the age of five and walked into the school with what I can only describe as a pimp roll. No more Osh Kosh dungarees – he'd have been dead on the streets of North London. It was my first sign of the persona boys feel they have to adopt to survive. Everything he had learned at home about being kind and gentle gave him no kudos. He had to be one of the boys, belonging to a posse. At this stage I could only talk to him about it, make it clear that there were values at home that I expected him to uphold. For myself, I have to achieve a delicate balancing act and accept that my child will lead a double life and have two personalities. One at home and one to fit in at school.'*

Richard's son, Nicholas, didn't suffer the same problems Ed did because of his dancing until he moved from junior to senior school. Then he began to be bullied and seriously teased for appearing to be somewhat effete. He became very unhappy and when Richard tried to involve the school there was very little change. In the end Nicholas solved the problem himself. Richard explains:

> 'I take my hat off to him. He went out one day and came home with his hair bleached absolutely white blonde. It was a shock when I saw it, but he went into school the next day and from that moment the bullying stopped. It was as if he'd just turned around and said "Fuck you all, I don't give a shit," and they admired him for it.'

Like Richard, Tariq Ali, the broadcaster and novelist, is also able to compare boys and girls being brought up in the same family. He has two daughters and a son and I asked him how easy was it to bring them up as equals?

> 'I find personally that my youngest daughter is far naughtier and more feisty. The contradiction is how to teach them – boys or girls – how to be 'normal' like everyone else and not feel out of place, and yet challenge the idea that boys will be boys. I remember one incident when my son was about five or six and two friends came round to play football. They kicked the ball to him and the ball lay at his feet and they said "Kick it" and he said "Why?"'

Tariq wasn't the slightest bit worried about his son's lack of interest in the sport, but then he's a man who has never had difficulties in displaying his 'feminine' side. He's at ease in the company of women, one of the great talkers of our time and a wickedly amusing raconteur and gossip. But the question of her son's inadequacy in the ball skills department was obviously of great concern to Melanie Cable-Alexander, a single mother whose son, Jasper, aged four, had a penchant for going to school in lip gloss but no interest whatsoever in football. She wrote of her plight in *The Daily Telegraph*:

> 'A sports mad male friend alarmed me when he relayed that "it is terribly important for boys to get their eye in for ball games from a very young age". I played netball at school and was captain of the rounders team, but I assumed that these were not the kind of games

*he was referring to – especially as he is of the robust view that all
boys belonging to single mothers are sissies and the best treatment
for them is to "pack them all off to boarding school to have some
stuffing knocked out of them".'*

*I read that single mothers with boys should beg and borrow guys
to play sports with their sons if they want them to turn out to be
well-rounded men. In his section on single mothers, Steve
Biddulph, author of* Raising Boys, *acknowledges: "There is no
doubt that women can raise good men (phew), but the ones I have
spoken to who succeeded always stress that they found good male
role models calling in help from uncles, good friends and so on."'*

She is right when she asserts in her article that it's around the age
of six that boys begin to differentiate between the sexes and look
for male role models to teach them about what it means to be
masculine. Interest is again aroused in the early teens, both occasions when testosterone rushes are affecting the body, and also
when differences between girls and boys are being emphasised in
the society around them (more on this in Chapter Five). Whilst
small babies and toddlers might escape the influences of gender
stereotyping, six-year-olds, who are beginning to look distinctly
more boyish and attending 'big' school, cannot. They're picking up
messages which may astonish the adults around them.

Cable-Alexander quotes a friend, also a single parent, who was
amazed by a conversation she had with her son. They often played
doctors and nurses together and he was usually the doctor. 'When
she recently suggested that she be the doctor for a change, Luke
looked appalled: "But Mummy you can't be the doctor because
you're a girl." She was flabbergasted. She works as a fully fledged
GP in Fulham.'

These stories re-emphasise the need for dialogue with even the
youngest children about the ideas they're picking up from outside.
What the article doesn't explain is what discussion the doctor had
with her son about the silly assumptions he made. Where had he
got the idea that women can't be doctors? What did he think
Mummy did when she went to work? It looks to me like the ideal
time to take her son to work and show him that both men and

women can be doctors. (I've never quite understood why we've had a Take Your Daughters to Work campaign and never extended the same invitation to our sons.)

As for the question of male role models, I don't deny that boys in single parent families need models of both sexes – indeed I'd extend that requirement to children in dual parent families as well – mine have benefited enormously from close relationships with adults from outside the family, both male and female, who've broadened their perspectives in myriad ways – but the choice of role models must be made with great care. We should never forget that people bring their own political prejudices about gender to bear on their dealings with children. It's important to find out where they're coming from – and just as my radical feminist friend who saw boys as the enemy would be far from ideal, so too would a man who displayed misogynist, anti-feminist or homophobic tendencies. Without doubt, a friend who thought boys needed to be sent to boarding school to be toughened up would not be my choice of candidate to offer guidance to a 'good' man in the making.

So what do we do about the potential battleground that sport has become? As in all these discussions, it seems to me vital that we relax about ridiculous pronouncements on what boys are supposed to like and dislike, get to know our own boys and allow them to lead the way. Some boys will absolutely adore playing football from the minute they learn to move around on two feet. India Knight's two boys are absolutely passionate about . . .

'Footy, rugby, cricket, tennis, martial arts, running around yelling at the top of their voices and slamming into furniture for no discernible reason . . . I have absolutely no interest in any sport whatsoever and just glaze over as some fabulous goal is re-enacted – one is the footballer, the other the crowd – for the nth time. Actually it makes me want to cry with boredom. But they have a father who played rugby as a child, a step-father who is a Celtic supporter, step-uncles ditto (they've learned some, er, interesting songs); and anyway I think it's healthy and good for them to have hobbies which don't include me.'

I, of course, share India's complete lack of interest in all ball games, but have, in Charlie's case, made a real effort to become a rugby mum. It mattered to me that he shouldn't see the game as an entirely male preserve – and some of the other mothers who go are genuinely interested in the matches, and some of the sisters play for their own girls' teams, so it's not quite the preserve it was. I have, of course, suffered for my ignorance of its finer points, but it became more important as Charlie got older – as he moved from junior to senior school – to be seen as a supporter of him, if not necessarily a fan of the game. I have grown to enjoy it more as I've begun to understand it better.

Charlie now, at the age of fifteen, can be dismissive of his need to have me there. He invariably walks off with his friends and barely acknowledges my presence, but I know he'd be disappointed if I ignored an activity, which is such an important part of his life. Jenny Stephen remembers her sons at around fifteen or sixteen announcing they didn't really want her to bother coming any more to watch them play sport. When she stopped going, they accused her of not being interested in them any more! Even now, she says, the older ones are keen sportsmen and, if she's around, are pleased when she manages to go along.

It is a pain in the neck having to get up at the crack of dawn on freezing winter mornings and drive around the country to stand on a touchline, but it has given me the opportunity to observe the ethos in which he's operating. I have at times registered my fury at referees, parents and coaches who've treated the boys with aggression and contempt, rather than teaching them about healthy competition and 'gentlemanly' behaviour in both victory and defeat.

The drive to and from the pitch is often a useful time for conversation – as indeed is the drive to and from school. Kids seem to value and use these occassions – when they have you captive on your own, but when your concentration is not entirely focussed on them – for bringing up issues which they may not communicate when other members of the family are around or when your attention is 'full on'. Some experts say boys need these opportunities more than girls, because face to face conversation is often not something that forms part of the culture they inhabit once they are away from home and out in the world.

Ed was never a keen ball player. He had a go at both football and rugby, but seems to have inherited my, rather than his father's, talent. I did, though, think it was important that he should take part in some physical pursuit, which would help keep him fit and use up his energy in a positive way. After Charlie was born, when Ed was four, it occurred to me that he and I should do something together which Charlie couldn't be a part of. It's terribly hard for any child to accept that a new baby has come into the family and displaced him or her – I always compare it with what it would be like if one's partner brought in a younger, cuter model and expected you to live alongside him or her – so I suggested to Ed that he might like to think of an activity that really grabbed him and it could be 'our' thing whilst Daddy looked after Charlie.

He said he'd like to take up riding (that love of animals again). I was hugely relieved, as it's the only sport I've ever enjoyed. We spent many happy hours at Wimbledon Village Stables sharing a passion for horses, riding out together, mucking out, grooming and cleaning tack. From his point of view it was a physical sport in which he delighted and for which he had a natural talent, inherited, I suspect, as was mine, from my grandfather who had joined the Royal Horse Artillery after being called up during the First World War, and had taken to being on horseback with ease.

It also gave Ed a social life outside school, which brought him into contact with lots of girls who shared his interest. When Charlie got older he began to ride too, as did David, so it became a family sport and social life, although the two of them were never quite as involved in the horsey scene as Ed and I were. But I'm convinced that one of the reasons my boys are now at ease in the company of women and girls results from the years they spent as young boys and early teenagers with girls who were friends and physical equals.

There can be real problems, though, for the boys who are not, as India describes her two, naturally 'boyish' about sport. They are the ones whose parents – often their dads – think they're not real mini-men unless their ambition in life is to be the next David Beckham. Diane Abbott remembers with horror how she struggled with her conviction that James should be involved in some sort of sport because she thought it was what boys did and she didn't want him to become a couch potato. With the help of her friend, the MP Jeremy Corbyn, she got him into the Arsenal kids football team. It was, she recalls, catastrophic:

'It was terrible. It was full of little boys with super ambitious dads and some of the boys were good and really LOVED football. James was always the last to be picked for the teams. On one occasion, someone kicked a ball at him and he just didn't move. He begged me not to go, he hated it so much, but I made him finish. I suppose it's because I'm a girl, I just didn't understand that there are some boys who really don't like that macho world of football. For a long time I thought it was all my fault, I'd made him too girly. Now I realise he's just a boy who doesn't like football. We finally hit on badminton and swimming. He's really good at both, keeps fit and enjoys himself.'

To those who still have doubts about whether it is vital for boys to become involved in the 'male' sports, I recommend Andy Miller's hilarious *Tilting At Windmills – How I Tried to Stop Worrying and Love Sport*. He eventually, as an adult, became a fanatical Crazy Golf player, but, as a child, he was that boy who never got picked for the team and never understood why sport was such a national obsession.

'I'm sorry this book has been such a long time coming, but I honestly thought someone else would write it first.

I hate sport.

I've always hated it.

I don't just mean one or two types of sport; I don't get any of them. I hate football. I don't understand cricket. Swimming leaves me cold. Rugby strikes fear into my heart. For something so dangerous, motor racing is unbelievably boring. I haven't got the balls for snooker. Darts is a drag. Athletics? I've got a note from my mum. Anyone for tennis? I'd rather stick needles in my eyes.

Saturday afternoons, the beautiful game, the roar of the crowd, the euphoria of victory, the humiliation of defeat, but knowing we'll be back next week, the hot pie in cold hands, the location of the *hamstring, that episode of* Whatever Happened to the Likely Lads? *where they try to avoid learning the result of the big match so they can watch it on TV later, all mean nothing to me.*

I don't even know why people throw Frisbees in the park on a sunny day.

Which is no mean feat when you think about it. I mean, this stuff is everywhere – if you're a man, more than everywhere. In your school, at work, on TV, on the radio, in newspapers, conversations with your mates, conversations with strangers, conversations with my mother (if the sport in question is golf), in the air, on the airwaves, in the atmosphere and stratosphere, we are all supposedly One Nation Under a Ball. The sporting life is the life of us all.

Well, not quite all. Whisper it, but many of us aren't really bothered. For all the thousands of people who can name the line-up of the 1966 World Cup Team, there are millions of us who can't. We have no idea what 'silly mid-on' means; we do not know the difference between rugbys, league and union; we would be unable to name three British tennis players if you put a gun to our heads (er, Henman, Rusedski, er . . . no, you're going to have to shoot me); we do not, essentially, care What Happened Next.

The 1990s, therefore, was not a good time for us. Sport for All became an order rather than a suggestion. We watched in horror as the UK's obsession with games passed into mania, becoming unapologetically middle class in the process. "It's in there all the time," says Nick Hornby, in the very first line of Fever Pitch, *referring to his love of football, "looking for a way out." Well, let it out, Nick, I say, let it out and be done with it. The rest of us could do with a break.'*

Andy's view is confirmed by Sam, one of the interviewees in Heather Formaini's book, Men – The Dark Continent, published in 1991. He had described how his father tried to 'train' him and instil in him a 'fighting masculinity', based on defence skills and tactics:

'It was repulsive to me, but I couldn't let my father know it and so I carried on with both sides of my life. One side of me hated what

*my father represented and wanted me to become, and the other side
of me pretended that I was just what he wanted. And so I would
play football even though I hated it. In fact I was much more interested in the kind of values my mother showed me.'*

The 'boys will be boys' phenomenon seems to have a particular
resonance when it comes to housework. I've already mentioned the
less than subtle ticking off Ed had at playschool, when he was
quietly occupied in the Home Corner and his play leader thought
he should be acting like a 'proper boy', climbing or playing with
cars. It's my suspicion that this prejudice is replicated in
playschools, nurseries and homes the country over, denying boys
the opportunity to become self-sufficient. Any opportunity to learn
at school, rather than later in life, has gone, too, as domestic
science or home economics have long since disappeared from the
school curriculum for both boys and girls; disastrously, in my view.

During my years of bringing up my own boys, I've been saddened
and surprised at the number of lovely lads who've come to our
house, been able to conduct an interesting conversation, play
quietly and creatively, sit with impeccably good manners at our
table, eat with gusto and then get up from the table and make off.
I can't count the number of times they've been on their way out of
the kitchen, leaving the debris of a recently consumed meal behind
them, when I'll yell, 'Oi! hold on a minute.' They'll stop, look back
and guiltily mumble. 'Oh, thank you, that was lovely.' 'That's not
what I'm talking about,' I'll say, 'you've already said thank you.
Now what do you do?' And they'll look at me blankly. When I
point out that dishes go in the dishwasher and left-overs in the bin
or the fridge, they'll happily pad about and get on with it with
affable good grace. The point is, it doesn't occur to them to clear
away as a matter of course. I've even heard from their mothers – on
the rare occasions I've ever been brave enough to mention their
beloved's inadequacies in the domesticity department; and if you
do it, you have to be light-hearted or you will quickly find you've
made formidable enemies of the mothers whose boys you dared to
criticise: 'Ah well, he's a boy isn't he? Just like his father, he doesn't
seem to notice what needs to be done!' Boys will be boys again,

letting them off the hook, and assuming that the condition of domestic blindness is incurable.

Of course he doesn't notice if it's never pointed out to him and if he's never expected to do his share. I become infuriated by these women who moan about their own husband's failure to pull his weight at home and then let their own sons get away with exactly the same behaviour – making, as I've said, a rod for some other poor woman's back.

All polls and surveys conducted into the area of domestic work in recent years have shown that the burden of labour within the home falls primarily on women. Typically wives do an average 90 per cent of the laundry and 82 per cent of all indoor cleaning and tidying. Even as greater numbers of women have begun to take their place in the workforce outside the home, the assumption that housework is women's work continues, but there's evidence that women are thoroughly fed up with the double shift they have to perform. A poll in the *New York Times* showed that only one in twenty women considered 'being a wife' to be one of the most enjoyable things about being female (well behind both career and motherhood). How many times have you heard a friend who goes out to work say, 'All I really need is a wife!'?

As women we want to have children, homes and fulfilling lives outside the home. We want husbands or partners who will be committed to caring for the nurture of our children for as long as they need it. No-one now disputes the fact that wherever possible children fare better emotionally and economically in households where safety, comfort and joy rule the roost rather than poverty, emotional deprivation and rancour. In her book *Wifework*, Susan Maushart pulls together the argument that some of us have been formulating for years:

> '*Women today initiate three quarters of all divorces and re-marry at less than half the rate of their ex-partners. Wifework lies at the core of this disillusionment. If family life is worth saving (and as I've said, generally speaking, the sensible among us agree that it is as, at its best, it nurtures men, women and children), Wifework will have to go. And that means re-writing the job description to*

make marriage more equitable, less exhausting and more fun for women . . . husbands and wives may say they are committed to equality. Yet, whether employed or not, wives still perform an astounding share of the physical, emotional and organisational labour in marriage.'

She quotes the views of a number of men about housework – one says he doesn't know how the bathroom gets cleaned, but, as it's always clean 'she must do it'. Another said, 'I do the washing up', but his wife added, 'He used to tell that to everyone and technically it was true. He did wash the dishes. What he didn't do was dry them or put them away. He also didn't wipe down the table, stove or bench top, sweep the kitchen floor, or clear away the leftovers.'

Maushart also looks at the reasons why women might now be choosing to remain single, even having children on their own without a resident father from the outset. We've all heard the young women, often so derided as simple seekers after a council flat, describe how they want a child – motherhood being the best way in which they can see themselves as having a useful future, given that for many working-class girls, as well as boys, the prospect of a career is a distant one – and explaining that they are prepared to look after the needs of one baby, but not two. In other words, they are not ready to mother their men. Maushart expresses it thus: 'To have babies without strings – i.e., men – attached is not simply a new lifestyle option. It is an unimaginably radical act of cultural subversion.'

If our boys are to have relationships in the future that are not stretched and broken on that rack of mismatched expectations; if they are not to be dismissed as worthless creatures for whom women are no longer prepared to care, we have to teach them now, as a matter of urgency, that the raising of children and management of a home are not Wifework, but the responsibility of everyone who needs to eat, wear clothes, use toilet paper, sleep on clean sheets, walk on clean floors etc, etc, etc, to muck in on an absolutely equal basis.

All the parents I've spoken to have taken on this subject, with varying degrees of success. India Knight has taken no prisoners on this one:

'Not an issue that's ever been up for debate, especially when I was single and hard up. They've always cooked and loved cooking – I get really demoralised at the idea that there are men around who can't feed themselves properly, so that was a deliberate thing from early on. They make their beds, tidy their rooms, help carry the shopping, pick up their stuff, pick up the dog's poo – with varying degrees of willingness, of course. Non-co-operation on this front is the one thing that would really make me go ballistic.'

In my family, too, everyone being part of the domestic life at home has always been a given. When the boys were very tiny, they were always around in the kitchen when we were cooking (note, when we were cooking – we never, as a couple, gave the impression that the kitchen was where Mummy functioned alone). They started with easy tasks like stirring and mixing, well away from danger areas such as stoves or kettles. They had simple children's cookbooks as soon as they were able to read and we made gingerbread men and butterfly cakes when friends were coming round to tea.

They had responsibility for laying the table, clearing up their own dishes and stacking the dishwasher – although I still, sometimes, have to remind them that it's OK to put the pots in the machine, rather than on the work surface over it. They've picked up from an early age the mantra that a good cook clears up as he or she goes along and that work surfaces and the space around the sink need to be wiped down every time. They don't always do it, especially if they've just been making toast, but then nobody's perfect, and, at least when they have their own kitchens to run they know the rules of basic hygiene. (Here I should give a word of praise to young Jamie Oliver, the TV chef who's done more to make cooking 'cool' for boys than any other single influence. My Ed cooked some brilliant onion rings on a recent holiday with the most delicious, light batter I've tasted since my grandmother's. Where had he got the recipe? Jamie Oliver!)

One of the most touching moments in all the years I've had my boys around started with a whispered, surreptitious phone call the day before their Dad's birthday when Ed was thirteen and Charlie nine. For the past nine years or so I've spent part of the week in

London for *Woman's Hour*, when Dave's been in sole charge at home. That year I wouldn't be back until the day after Dave's birthday, and the boys wanted to make a cake themselves.

They'd manage to 'blague' a couple of pounds to buy a Jane Asher chocolate mix on a trip to the supermarket, on the pretext of buying themselves some sweets. It was now ten o'clock at night, Dad had gone to bed and thought they were both fast asleep, and they were ready to bake the cake, but . . . disaster . . . the recipe required an egg and we didn't have any in the house. Would it be OK to nip next door to our neighbour whose smallholding has the most prolific chickens in the area and ask her for an egg, and would I please pay for it when I got home because they didn't have any more money? The cake was ready and waiting the next morning at breakfast, with the words 'Happy Birthday Dad' on top, cut out in cardboard, and one scruffy candle culled from the bottom of our notoriously overstuffed kitchen drawers. I have never heard a man so touched and thrilled as when he called to tell me what they'd done, and wondered how they'd managed to get away with it without him noticing. And who says teenage boys only think of themselves?

Jenny and Martin Stephen also included their boys in the preparation of food and basic household tasks, believing it important that they should understand about the benefits of good nutrition from an early age, so that when they finally left home, they would be able to look after themselves cheaply and without resorting to MacDonalds or Pizza Express. Jenny too started them out with simple tasks like stirring cakes and licking the bowl as a reward, then gradually progressing to more complicated fare. Jenny is also a keen gardener and encouraged the boys to join her in growing vegetables. They loved getting dirty when they were little and watching things come up. She would send them out to dig potatoes and pick fruit and vegetables for meals. Again, making them aware that 'five fruit and veg' a day is good for health became part of an activity that was fun. All three boys are now very good cooks.

Our constant vigilance has given rise to a few jokes, because our boys know exactly how to send Mum flying up to the ceiling.

Q: Why has no woman ever been to the moon?
A: It doesn't need dusting.
Q: How many husbands does it take to change a lightbulb?
A: None. She can cook in the dark.
Q: Why do women have small feet?
A: So they can fit under the cooker.
Q: Why do women get married in white?
A: Aren't all kitchen appliances white goods?

I've always handled these kind of blatantly sexist jokes by laughing, if they're funny. No-one wants to pander to the old chestnut that feminists have no sense of humour.

I then growl with mock irritation and respond with my own joke that turns the tables on them. Jeremy Paxman's e-mail has provided a fund of them, ever since he told a few dumb blonde jokes in public.

Q: How many honest, intelligent, caring men does it take to do
       the dishes?
A: Both of them.
Q: Why does it take one million sperm to fertilise one egg?
A: They won't stop and ask for directions.
Q: How many men does it take to change a roll of toilet paper?
A: We don't know, it's never happened.
Q: Why are married women heavier than single women?
A: Single women come home, see what's in the fridge and go
       to bed. Married women come home, see what's in the bed
       and go to the fridge!

There's only one sexist/domestic joke they've ever told me that I really didn't find funny and insisted they shouldn't tell – not in our house anyway.

Q: What do you do if your washing machine breaks down?
A: Slap her.

Domestic violence is never acceptable, even though, on the surface the joke might seem amusing.

Housework in general – washing, ironing, tidying up – is also something we've always been careful to portray as a joint responsibility – although we have usually had a cleaner who's come in a couple of times a week to help out. I've been insistent that the boys sort out their own laundry, putting dirty clothes in the basket and freshly ironed ones away.

Richard Denton was quite wry when I asked him about his children's contribution to the domestic life of the household and whether there was any difference in the attitudes of the boy and the girl.

'No distinction. Neither does anything. Although when we were building a new kitchen, she was more useful – she was definitely more interested in DIY. They've always had responsibilities for cleaning, cooking and washing for as long as I can remember, but they're both clumsy, neither is adept, things get broken and baths overflow. I guess they're just careless, but, then, I'm not such a great role model. I tend to tackle it in splurges, but I do insist that certain things are necessary just to avoid being rude. For instance, if I've taken the trouble to iron their clothes, I do expect them to take the trouble to put everything away in their drawers.'

When my two were small it was all very easy and part of the games we played. They had their own little hoovers – push alongs, which actually worked – and they never baulked at joining in. For a long time it was fun and a good way of carrying out those sideways conversations about what they'd been up to all day – a time when my concentration was not obsessively focussed on them, and I'd get to hear much more than if I'd sat them down at the kitchen table and quizzed them.

As they get older, it becomes more difficult. Messy rooms for both genders seem to be a classic form of rebellion during the teenage years and their solution, which Linda Bellingham, like me, experienced with her older boy (her younger one is naturally tidier) is to ban mothers from the bedroom, assuming that if it's all hidden behind a closed door, you won't even notice it. Linda, like me, found it a constant source of rows and arguments.

'I tried very hard to bring them up to be amazing blokes who would cook and wash up and be caring. They had dolls when they were little and hoovers and cookers. My sister has two girls, so she gave

them the same presents. It was a bit pointless, but then I had all that Italian influence to deal with from their Dad and his side of the family. Men there definitely rule the roost and don't expect to have to do anything. It's very hard when they're getting mixed messages.

It really did become a problem with Michael who would always say, "I'll do it later" and just didn't seem to understand why I could be annoyed about it if I couldn't see it. I did point out that it was something I was aware of and it irritated me, but he couldn't seem to get it. I also wasn't entirely happy with the idea that his room was totally off limits to me. You need to enter the portals occasionally, just to make sure they're not storing an arsenal or a stash of drugs in there. It caused a lot of friction. Now he's partly left home and is living with his girlfriend, I discover he actually cleans her flat for her. When I questioned him about it, I was pretty annoyed because it seemed so unfair to me; he grinned and said "Well, I'm not shagging you, Mum". I suppose some of it got through, then!'

It does get through, but it is another area when Dads or a close male friend need to be on board to do some pestering. There's nothing worse than Mum being forced to take on the role of 'nag'. I don't believe in bribery. Paying boys to do essential jobs around the house suggests they're employed to do them as a favour. It's much better if housework is simply a responsibility or a necessary evil to which every member of the family is expected to contribute. Nothing annoys me more than the idea that boys or husbands are 'a help' around the house. Don't give them the impression that it's really the woman's job and their contribution is just being helpful. It is EVERYBODY'S job.

If you do have a cleaner and the boys insist on leaving their clothes and mess on the bedroom floor, waiting for the cleaner to clear up after them, point out that you pay her to clean the house, not tidy up outrageous mess. If that doesn't do the trick, deduct a portion of the cleaner's wages from their pocket money. It's the kind of punishment that really works. They'll soon start clearing up.

Some parents have complained to me that their boys seem hopelessly disorganised during the teenage years, and getting ready for school in the morning can be a nightmare. Where are my socks, where's my shirt, where are my specs? I can't find my English book! Sit them down and explain the importance of forward planning, perhaps getting everything ready the night before and keeping school necessities in an ordered fashion. If that doesn't work, do nothing. If they faff about and miss the school bus, they'll be late. If they haven't got the right homework book or sports kit, they'll be in trouble. Let the school take the strain. A few lines, detentions or tickings off from the rugby coach soon sets them straight and let's you right off the hook!

CHAPTER THREE

BIG BOYS DON'T CRY

A couple of years ago I chaired an extraordinary conference for the Child Bereavement Trust. Its aim was to inform teachers and other professionals of the importance of recognising emotional distress in a child who has lost a parent or a brother or sister, and to give them strategies for supporting the children. What was most astonishing about the day's events was the appearance of Bill Morris, General Secretary of the Transport and General Workers Union (TGWU), and one of the toughest negotiators in the business. It was the first time I had attended such an event, and heard a successful man – known in politics for his hard-headed and cool approach – stand up and bring an audience to tears with an emotional outburst.

Morris talked about his memories of losing his father when he was a boy of fifteen in the Caribbean. His father was taken ill suddenly and Bill was sent to fetch the medicine the doctor had prescribed. When he arrived back at home his father was dead. Bill was racked with guilt. If only he'd run a bit faster, would his father have survived? He lived in an involved community with a large matriarchal extended family, so there were plenty of people around who expressed their grief openly, but Bill was told only that he shouldn't cry and that he was now the head of the household.

It was an intolerable burden to place upon a young boy and it was obvious from what Bill said in his speech that the sense of responsibility imposed on him and the demand that he repress his sadness in order to prove himself a man had blighted his entire emotional life. We might think our fifteen-year-olds are adults, but they are not; it's at this period in their lives that they are learning how to break away and become their own man and they need to learn, just as they have through their lives up to teenage, how to express their hurt, upset and joy. We will not help them grow into men who can express their feelings to their wives, partners and children if we tell them at these vulnerable moments that Big Boys Don't Cry.

Part of the problem, of course, is that our boys are being raised in a social environment that still seems to refuse to believe that men have feelings. Their grandfathers and great-grandfathers were often terribly damaged by the wars of the twentieth century, survived with a stiff upper lip and, as a result, frequently remained distant from their families for the rest of their lives. There appears to be a terrible reluctance on the part of those old men to discuss with their sons and grandsons the awful emotional scarring that damaged their own relationships for a lifetime.

I remember when Charlie was about seven he asked one of his grandfathers, who had seen action in the Second World War, what it felt like to kill someone. His question was brushed aside with the dismissive comment, 'We don't talk about that sort of thing'. I was in no position to argue, not wanting to step on any family toes, but I now regret it. It's surely the duty of old men to tell the young how ghastly it really is to point a gun at another man and see him fall, and to describe what dies in the perpetrator when he's done it. How else are we to counter the glamorised images of guns and battles with which the young are constantly fed by the media?

Boys have always suffered from a parlous lack of advice and information about how to deal with powerful feelings and teenage angst, as they have been shortchanged when it comes to realistic or rounded heroes. I have been hard pressed to find any comics or magazines for boys which don't concentrate almost exclusively on outdoor pursuits, superheroes, comic cuts, cars and sport. Girls, by contrast, have, for at least a century, been fed a regular diet of reading matter, which has nurtured their emotional lives and given them a range of inspirational role models to follow.

When Mel Gibson, a researcher from the University of Sunderland, wrote her PhD on the influence of girls' comics, such as *Girl* and *Schoolfriend*, *Bunty* and *Jackie*, she found plenty of examples of sheer comedy, such as my favourite, Lettice Leefe, the Greenest Girl in the School, but there were also admirable figures like the Four Marys and any number of girl characters with aspirations to become professional women. As Gibson says:

> *'There were tales of solidarity, of girls being adventurous, of strong central characters in command. You had to be able to talk your way out of things in a girls' comic, you could not solve plot difficulties by blowing someone's head off.'*

Equally magazines aimed at girls have always brimmed with information about everything, from how to deal with the first spot to how to survive your parents' splitting up. Boys have had no such support. Indeed when I suggested some years back to a leading publisher of materials for girls and young women that they should do something similar for boys as an antidote to the dreadful 'lad mags', such as *Loaded* and *FHM*, which were being bought by boys well below the age group for which they were intended, I was told, 'No point, boys don't read'.

It seems some people even find it hard to accept that boys have any concerns about their appearance, despite growing evidence that rising numbers are as body obsessed as girls are. Specialists in eating disorders are beginning to see more boys than ever before, the search for the 'six pack' has become an obsession with large numbers of boys and, at the first sign of body hair, they're beginning to ask themselves whether they should go off for the 'back, sack and crack' – I don't need to spell it out I'm sure, but it involves wax, a beauty salon and an awful lot of pain.

There is some consolation in the long-term future for boys who suffer from eating disorders. Work carried out by Dr Emily Lovegrove at the Centre for Appearance Research at the University of the West of England indicates that boys' problems tend not to last as long as those suffered by girls. Whereas girls who grow into women see themselves becoming fatter and losing the boyish figure they crave, boys grow into their cultural norm. They regain their confidence as they become taller and more muscular.

But despite all the evidence that boys are hungry for advice about their appearance and care just as much as girls about it, there's still an assumption that it doesn't really matter to them. When Charlie was involved in a nasty car accident and scarred his forehead badly, numerous people, even the lawyers involved in his compensation claim said, 'Oh, well, not to worry, at least he's only a boy!'

The limited range of subject matter available in publications for boys over the past century would be laughable if it weren't so tragic. In *The Best of British Pluck – The Boys Own Paper Revisited* by Philip Warner in 1976 (sent to me by Geoff Fox, a specialist in children's literature and the author with Kate Agnew of *Children at War from the First World War to the Gulf*), there's a selection of the kind of advice doled out by the editor, G. A. Hutchinson, in the period from 1879 to 1913. In answer to the question, 'Why was it necessary to have a medical examination for the armed forces?', he replied:

> 'The object of the medical examination is that the country should not be served by the deformed, the crippled and the weak. If you are not perfect in limb and health, you are simply wasting your time. Is it likely that a lad with a broken leg and a hip growing out would make a desirable soldier?'

His attitude to corporal punishment was to treat it as a joke.

> 'The recipient may be discouraged from repeating the offence, although some might transgress again out of sheer bravado. It is preferable to a lengthy imposition. A boy's first beating is an initiation ceremony. You cannot command respect until you have taken six of the best without flinching. In the same way a soldier is not a soldier until he has been on a 'charge' and duly punished.'

There were queries even then about superfluous hairs:

> 'We cannot advise the use of depilatories. They increase the hair's growth as certainly as the razor does. They do NOT destroy the root, whatever ladies' newspapers who take quack advertisements may say to the contrary.'

Boys were generally given advice along the lines that just as animals should be well looked after, so boys should take cold baths, exercise vigorously with dumbbells and stop visiting art galleries, if troubled by sexual thoughts. 'The cold bath will form you up. Playing cricket one day a week is nothing. Exercise must be taken every day.' The editors of *Boys Own*, *Chums* and *The Captain* were generally agreed that 'tak[ing] a cold bath' was the cure-all for any evil, with the qualification, 'Do not make more splash than you can help so as not to trouble the servants'.

There was certainly no time for the 'emotional' boy. 'Anxious', aged thirteen got a very straight answer.

> *'Anxious asks, does the heart really get affected in any way when we sympathise with a person? Is it the brain alone that controls the actions? You are no fool, Arthur, though but thirteen. There is a most intimate sympathy between the brain and the heart and between mind and matter. The emotional heart is a feeble heart and this is often somewhat en rapport with a somewhat excitable brain. As men grow older and the heart gets feebler, they become more sympathetic. A coward never has a strong heart, so cowardice in boys or men is really a disease.'*

As the magazines were concerned to 'make upstanding Britons' of the boys who read them, in the comics too, among the naughty boys and outrageous strongmen, such as Dennis the Menace and Desperate Dan, the stories were about action, adventure and toughening up. In *The Victor* from the 1950s onwards, the seminal boys' comic, there were always 'True Stories of Men at War' where German soldiers died screaming 'Arch!', whilst Japanese soldiers let loose with 'Aileen!!'. The formula was Football Story, War Story, War Story, Sport Story, and Fantasy Story. The characters were Morgyn the Mighty, Braddock VC and The Tough of The Track. Girls, apart from Beryl the Peril and Minnie the Minx, where entirely absent.

Similarly, when it comes to literature, boys seem hardly to have been touched by the classic novelists, such as Jane Austen, who examined relationships between men and women and the gender politics of their time. Dr Gillian Lacey from the National Centre for Research into Children's Literature at the University of Surrey in Roehampton, cites novels, like Thomas Hughes' *Tom Brown's Schooldays, By An Old Boy,* as typical fare. It was published in 1857, but set at Rugby School in the 1830's, just after William Webb Ellis, the inventor of modern rugby would have graduated. In it Hughes describes the 'classic' schoolboy:

> *'It's very odd how almost all English boys love danger; you can get ten to join a game or climb a tree or swim a stream, when there's a chance of breaking their limbs or getting drowned, for one who'll stay on level ground, or in his depth or play quoits or bowls.'*

Dr Lacey describes Hughes' novel as 'typical literary fare for boys across the generations'. It is, she says, 'Full of muscular Christianity, of playing the game, obeying the rules, displaying one's manliness and protecting the weak. A tall order for boys to live up to.'

There are some hints that things may be changing. The very magazine publisher who told me boys don't read was quoted in a recent article as saying, 'A lifestyle magazine for teenage boys is the publisher's Holy Grail'. The excellent *Sunday Surgery* on Radio One on Sunday nights is proving that he may be right and that boys' hunger for help and advice is finally finding an outlet. The programme, aimed at young people between the ages of fifteen and twenty-four, is presented by one of the station's sparkiest DJ's, Emma B and Doctor Mark Hamilton. Calls and e-mails from boys and young men have risen considerably in the months since the programme started three years ago. The gender of the listeners is split 50/50, but the percentage of males responding to the helpline number has increased to 65 per cent. They regularly take calls dealing with everything from bullying to bereavement and bad breath.

Among the most touching calls heard in recent weeks was one from a young man who had just gone to university and was desperately lonely. He spoke about how much he was still grieving for his father who had died two years ago. It was obviously the first time he had spoken about it. The producer, Sam Steele, tells me that one recent call, which moved them, was from a young soldier who went AWOL from his unit because he was terrified of being sent to the Gulf. He was calling from his car where he had been living for two weeks.

She has also noticed an increasing articulacy when talking about feelings and relationships. The worries that are expressed in the calls and e-mails are often about becoming more emotionally involved with their girlfriends and partners than the girls seem to want. One e-mailer whose girlfriend of five years was cooling off wrote:

'I love her with all my heart and I always will. Then last week we decided to call it a day. It was a decision made by both of us. She said she wanted us to be good friends, but I have not heard from her since last week. I wrote her a letter the other day, telling her what my feelings were, but I have not had any response from her. It is tearing me apart, because I am thinking that I made a big mistake by agreeing to part. How can I tell her how I am feeling and get a response from her? Please help!'

A sixteen-year-old, clearly troubled by dreadful guilt, wrote:

'My friend died last year after taking LSD and jumping from a balcony. I feel I could have stopped him if I'd been there. I'm at boarding school and don't feel I can trust any of the staff to keep what I say confidential.'

And when the programme discussed testicular cancer, they were inundated with grateful e-mails from young males who obviously hadn't a clue about how their own bodies functioned or what services were available to them. This humorous comment from one young listener was typical:

'Thanks . . . for the show. If I didn't listen, then I wouldn't have had the balls – no pun – to go to the A & E yesterday to have a check-up when I found a lump. I now have to wait for a scan result, but boy am I glad that you guys put the message out. Keep it up. Andrew.'

Sam says the most significant change she has noticed in the time she has been involved with the programme was apparent in a call received from thirteen-year-old Chris in Stirling. He wanted advice about dating a friend of his. They had already been out together, but split up because they thought they were better as friends. Chris, though, still wanted more from the relationship and wondered whether he should ask her out again, but didn't want to ruin the friendship. He had already discussed the situation with his male friends and they had told him not to do anything, but he wanted Emma's and Mark's opinion too. Sam thinks this is very rare – for a boy to have discussed it with his mates before calling in – and thinks it may point to a future where boys begin to lose their inhibitions about exposing their emotional side to each other (more on *Sunday Surgery* in Chapter Four).

Childline in 1996 noted a rise in the number of boys calling for help, reported in Simon Forrest's paper 'Boys learning about sexuality and manhood'. Boys called about domestic violence, offending and school worries, and a disproportionately high number seemed worried about sexuality, drug use and abusing other children. However, of all calls, only 18 per cent came from boys. It's said they talk less when they call, are less fluent and easy, and are highly self-critical of having to seek help at all, giving the impression they still believe that 'Real boys don't feel'. The researchers – Macleod and Barter – concluded that:

> *'Boys feel barred from talking because talk does not fit with their ideals of manhood, which run along the lines of "Boys act strong; it's soft to ask for help; boys have to be tough; girls are more sensitive; boys find it embarrassing and think it's their fault". Helping boys is important for their future behaviour as men, fathers and family members.'*

In *Men*, published thirteen years ago, Heather Formaini gathered ample evidence from adult males of how the Big Boys Don't Cry philosophy had affected the generation of men who were in their twenties and thirties in the late 1980's and 1990's; young men who had great concerns about how they might break out of the cycle for the benefit of their own sons.

In her chapter on the meaning of masculinity, Formaini describes having observed in all her interviewees a conflict between being a masculine man and being his own individual self. The men seem, she says, to get caught up in being like other men – one of the boys – and following the rigid rules of masculinity which dictate every step of the way from infancy to death. And it is this process which, Formaini believes, takes away their individuality. Her thesis has strong echoes for anyone who has studied feminist theory or for any woman or girl who has been raised in the past fifty years.

We know only too well the constraints of the rules of femininity which dictated our duties, our appearance and our behaviour and, whilst giving us permission to feel, frequently frowned upon us as soft or hysterical. We've fought very hard as a collective movement to break out of those rules and in some ways it has been easy for us. The characteristics we questioned – whether as women we were naturally more emotional, destined to serve the opposite sex and to confine ourselves to the domestic sphere – were characteristics that were generally undervalued; while the qualities we were determined to acquire – associated with strength, power and praise for our contribution to the world outside the home – were qualities generally considered commendable.

For boys there seems to be no greater fear than being seen as feminine, and I guess it hasn't really been in the interests of the group that conventionally held the power to plot to weaken their position. So men were encouraged, as David, one of Formaini's interviewees explains, to suppress any aspect of their natural personality that might be seen as girlie. He remembers as a very young boy being taken aside by his father and told to behave in a different way:

'If I am a little boy, I have to cut off everything that means being a little girl. I don't cry any more, I keep a stiff upper lip, and I pretend I like games even if I am terrible at them and I am stoic and all that sort of stuff. I'm talking about all the things I had to give up. All the things that were considered soppy were to do with my feelings. It was my little boyness which actually disallowed me from expressing feelings. I think it's largely conditioning. I remember being a very affectionate rather sentimental little boy, and then, my father, with

whom I had a very good relationship, said, "Well, you're a big boy now and that means you don't cry and you don't kiss me goodbye at the station." And so it was the instruction: Don't show feelings.'

David has no doubt that his suppression of his feelings has had a severe impact on his ability to form successful, close and intimate relationships with women.

'No, I don't do it. I get prickly. An image that comes to mind is of a strange crustacean creature in Hieronymous Bosch's Garden of Earthly Delights; and I think, that's me, a prickly crustacean.'

Another of Formaini's interviewees, Richard, a lawyer in his early thirties, remembered how the observation of the rules of masculinity was strictly enforced at school.

'Men have assumed these characteristics – the hard role, no feelings – for so long, that their characters start to change. Probably from as early as boys start to form images of the world, they have to stifle, whether they realise it or not, those more sensitive feelings. Though they always remain, you have to pretend otherwise, and that makes it harder to reveal them.'

Philip, a forty-five-year-old architect, was also struggling with the pressure his father had put upon him from a very young age not to show his emotions and to be 'strong and an achiever':

'I resent quite a lot the need to achieve. I was conditioned by my father who said, "Find a niche, stick to it and be a good lad and find a steady job." And I've done it. I also have the job he wanted to have. But I feel excluded by being a man – excluded from the human race. Women find it very difficult to understand this is how men live their lives: there's a work compartment, there's a home compartment and there are other compartments – and they are not related. So when you're in one, you're not in another. For instance it's quite difficult in the office to get a call from a lover, because it's one compartment coming into another. The person I am at work is

quite different from the one at home. I know what I have to do at work. I am being paid to do certain things and I set out to do them. At work there is the strong bit; in my private life there is the floppy bit.'

Formaini's conclusion about what we do to our boys if we deny them an emotional life is profoundly sad and depressing:

'What seems clear from my personal observations, as well as the research material, is that boys are damaged from early on in life. It is almost possible to say that society requires them to be damaged so that they can carry on the tasks that society expects of them – to work and to be profitable and to uphold the male systems which have been in place for what must be thousands of years. But it cannot in any way benefit society if about half its members are damaged to the extent where they are split from their essential selves. By labelling some people feminine and others masculine we are forced to divide up human qualities into two categories. Invariably some qualities have been labelled 'good' and some 'bad'. We fall into a trap which prevents us becoming individual persons with real human qualities.'

Yet ideas about keeping a stiff upper lip and suppressing emotions persist. A year before the Bereavement conference, in May 1999, Professor Richard Harrington, a child psychiatrist at the University of Manchester had made headlines with his contention that counselling bereaved children did more harm than good. He claimed that children are resilient, and suggested there was no evidence to show that a death in the family has a detrimental effect on the emotional development of a child or young person. I wish he'd been at the conference to hear Bill Morris.

There were some delegates who were ready to dismiss Bill's experience as coming from another era when feelings were swept under the carpet, arguing that things are not like that any more. But the young people, especially the boys, I've spoken to who have suffered the death of someone close to them indicate that very little has really changed. Their ages range from six to sixteen, and they all have difficult questions about what death meant, where the parent had gone, whether it was alright to wear a mother's scarf in order to feel close to her, why it was so difficult to talk to the surviving parent about it and what was going to happen to them? It's obvious to me that schools, parents and grandparents, need to nurse boys of all ages through the various stages of grief and to give them a chance to talk about what concerns they have; and remember that our boys are children who need reassurance and security, they are not mini-men who are ready to take on responsibility.

Similarly, there is patently a lack of attention paid to boys during that other life shattering set of circumstances faced by so many children – divorce. Jenny and Martin Stephen, in their capacity as teachers rather than parents of sons, have observed a different climate in recent years and agree that boys are infinitely more sensitive than they were ten years ago. It could be that they both run schools where the pastoral care of boys is considered as important as their intellectual development, so the atmosphere is one in which boys are encouraged to discuss their worries and anxieties about a range of subjects – from bullying to what's going on at home – with sympathetic members of staff.

It could also be that in the best schools there are lessons where these kind of issues are talked about. Both Jenny and Martin have found that boys in the upper forms are unsure about their role and are prepared to articulate their concerns. The change could, of course, be simply the result of wider cultural changes – it's now OK, as I'll explain later in this chapter, for boys to listen to advice programmes on the radio or to watch soaps like *Hollyoaks* or *East Enders* where what men and women, boys and girls feel is daily fare. Nevertheless, Jenny and Martin both report feeling absolute horror at the number of parents on the point of separation who have appeared in front of them and explained that the school really ought to know what is going on in the marriage, but the head teacher shouldn't worry, as the boy won't be affected – he's strong, he's tough, and he's not bothered, they say.

Jenny and Martin fume at such dismissals of the impact of painful experiences at home, particularly on boys. Jenny says she rarely hears parents talk of their girls in such a way. Both head teachers comment on a strange climate in which parents are, on the one hand, often more over-protective of their boys than they used to be, restricting their freedoms and their opportunities to test themselves against the world outside, because of fear of violence on the streets, but, at the same time, failing to accept that boys can be profoundly hurt and damaged by events which threaten their security.

Martin describes such behaviour as 'emotionally and intellectually stopping them getting dirty and developing an immune system'. He's worried that it creates an atmosphere where a boy can go completely off the rails. This is of particular concern during the most vulnerable time between thirteen and sixteen, which Martin describes as hormonally like being

> 'bounced along very fast down a tunnel. The light isn't obvious for quite a long time and the edges of the tunnel are extremely rough. Most boys of this age will be unhappy and find life very hard, just as they are coming up to tough exam times, and it really doesn't help if parents assume it's normal for teenagers to be miserable and they'll just come through it naturally. Some will, but a lot won't.'

There is an important lesson here for parents. Whether the boy is six or sixteen, he will be deeply affected by trouble at home. It appears that one of the hardest things for boys to deal with is, as I've already observed, that it is often the women who initiate divorce because they are disappointed in the ability of the men they married to take a full part in the emotional and practical areas of family life. Girls probably suffer less when divorce happens, because the females in the family can get together and will frequently collude in moaning together about Dad's shortcomings, but it's very confusing for a boy, especially during the teenage years when he's looking to his father for clues about how to be male, for Dad to be portrayed as a bastard. It's equally damaging for his mother to be described by the father as a vengeful bitch.

Angela Phillips in *The Trouble With Boys* quotes a study on the effects of divorce carried out in 1982, which showed a clear gender difference in the expectations of boys' and girls' reactions:

'"Crying and distress in boys received less frequent and shorter periods of comforting and more ambivalent comforting than did distress signals from girls." By "ambivalent" the researchers meant responses such as "a hug, combined with: there, there! Boys don't cry". Girls were far more likely to be given unqualified reassurance. The fact is, there is no socially sanctioned way in which boys can show their anxiety and ask for help. If they are rough and anxious, they are seen as aggressive, but they are given precious little encouragement to show weakness either. While girls are encouraged to seek help from adults, boys are expected to learn to cope. This encouragement may, again, not be explicit, but it is worth noting that girls and boys get different responses both to aggressive behaviour and to defensive behaviour.*

Little girls quickly learn that by crying they will enlist adult help on their side. Crying is therefore a more effective defence than hitting back. It might be in the interests of boys to learn the same strategy, but too often crying in boys will elicit a very different and far less positive response.'*

I've seen so many boys, friends of my own sons, pulled this way and that by warring parents. In one family where the father lived and worked abroad, the boy came close to a nervous breakdown and had to take a significant time away from school after his return from spending the summer with his father, unable to face his mother's constant censure of the Dad who had given him nothing but fun during the vacation. In another case, a male acquaintance told me recently that his sixteen-year-old had come back to live with him, ten years after his divorce, without telling his mother, who had simply 'got on his nerves'. The father told me this story with an air of triumph. He had 'won' his son back.

We all know divorce is painful for everyone concerned, and boys will not ride it unaffected. It's essential that parents act like adults for the sake of their boys, constantly aware that the way they portray the gender roles will have an effect on their son's development and on the way he may see himself as a man.

A small boy will need lots of cuddles and sensitive explanations about what is going on, along with reassurance that both Mum and

Dad have his interests at heart, that the problems are not his fault and that he will continue to have a relationship with both parents (more on Dads' involvement after divorce or separation in Chapter Seven).

Older boys need to know they are loved by both parents, too, and should never be used as weapons between factions who are kicking over the traces of a dead relationship. They need careful explanation of what has gone wrong. Here I'm talking about those divorces in which there may simply have been a growing apart, a new relationship outside the marriage or a dissatisfaction with the way the family works. (I'll deal with domestic violence in Chapter Five). What the sons need is reassurance that they are not to blame and comfort without qualification if they cry. Equally, they need lots of affection and attention from both parents, but especially they need to talk sensibly, calmly and rationally about gender roles in these circumstances. Nothing is more destabilising than sweeping arguments and feelings under the carpet, leaving children with guilt and ignorance. If, for instance, there has been an unfair division of labour, which the mother has finally decided is unacceptable, then both parents need to discuss the problems with their son and explain why the difficulties arose without making him feel that the divorce is about men being bad and women better. Nevertheless, fathers may well have to take responsibility for explaining what went wrong, perhaps apologising for their lack of attention to the domestic side of life and acknowledging that it isn't unmanly to clean a loo or cook supper (more of this in Chapter Seven).

The way matters are handled will impact, not only on his immediate future as a schoolboy, but on his long-term prospects as a man who is able or otherwise to form loving and mutually supportive relationships with women. Best of all, of course, and again this does not apply if there has been violence in the home, is for the parents to spend time talking to each other and trying to resolve their differences with the aim of staying together. The grass is so rarely greener on the other side and our boys' sense of well-being and security is surely more important than having a new love affair or resolving who washes the kitchen floor.

It's not always easy to talk with older boys. Even with those who have been raised in a family where discussion of feelings has never been repressed, there comes an age, around twelve or thirteen, when your articulate, funny little chap suddenly turns into Harry Enfield's Kevin the Teenager and either grunts or says, 'It's so unfair!'. The phase lasts in my experience for about three deeply frustrating years. Girls go through it, too, by the way, but seem to find it easier to chatter among their peer group, whereas, as I said in Chapter Two, even small boys seem to pick up on a 'male' culture they encounter outside the home where talking face to face is not encouraged. Which is why it's important that as parents we're open to conversation at times when we seem to be doing something else – driving, cooking or cleaning the house.

Many's the occasion on which I've asked both my sons directly, 'What did you do at school today?', and been treated to that catch-all negative response, 'Nothing much'. Other direct questions get a 'Yeah right', or 'Whatever!', or just that familiar grunt. There have been times when I have felt like a creature from another planet as the only female in the family when all three of them have gone into 'bloke' mode and I've felt very lonely as they josh and mutter at each other, excluding me from masculine forms of communication which I just don't understand. I've often tried to get in by asking questions, only to be told, 'Stop asking so many questions'; and our level of conversation has at times deteriorated to the level of nagging: 'Why haven't you tidied your room?', 'Why are you watching too much telly?', 'Why haven't you cleared up the dishes from the table?' Mum cast as nag is not a happy position to be in.

I realised that some of the tricks I use when I'm interviewing people to encourage them to open up might just produce less intim-idating opening gambits, hopefully resulting in more articulate and informative answers. A little tease, perhaps, as when I interviewed Dawn French recently and hoped she'd talk about her marriage to Lennie Henry. I opened with a bit of fun about her appearance on *Parkinson* during which she kissed George Clooney not once, but twice. It broke the ice. So a playful suggestion like, 'Let me guess what you did today?' should encourage a small child to think of conversation as a game. A friendly observation like, 'Blimey, you look whacked out, sweetheart', delivered with part grimace, part grin can often open the floodgates of a day's troubles with an older boy. Closed questions, such as 'Did you do your homework?', will most likely elicit a 'yes' or 'no'. More open questions, like 'How did you get on with your homework?', leave it open for him to explain. By contrast, 'Why did you do your homework like that?', and all similar 'why' questions are generally to be avoided, as there's a hint of criticism in the way the question is framed – guaranteed to get any boy to shut up like a clam.

I'm not usually persuaded by rules that are created to aid human communication, but reflective listening is one trick I've tried which does seem to work. Again, it's something I've used occasionally as an interviewer on those heart-stopping occasions when the interviewee completely loses track of what they are saying or forgets what the question was. It requires careful and attentive listening on my part – which, of course, helps more than anything with boys, as they always accuse parents of not listening to their opinions, so it's a good skill to develop as a parent. The way it works is to repeat what the person has just said. With interviewees it kick-starts the thought process which had temporarily escaped them and allows them to pick up where they left off without feeling foolish. With boys (and possibly girls, too, although I have no experience of them), it seems to give them cues and space and a comfortable atmosphere in which to articulate what they're thinking.

So, if your son says, 'There's no point in talking to you about this, because no one ever takes any notice of what I think', you can reply, 'Nobody takes any notice of you, so you'd like me to'. More often than not he'll say, 'Yes, I've got a lot to tell you'. That's when you sit down and listen, without making comment. It's hard to bite your tongue and not give advice. It can feel very awkward to speak to them in a way that doesn't marry with the natural pattern of conversation, but it can be very useful, especially if you suspect they are going through a difficult patch. They must always know that no matter how big, strong and male they think they have to be outside, the home is where it's OK to expose yourself. As parents we have to take great care always to be people that our sons can trust completely, never belittling or calling them 'soft' or 'soppy'.

They should be able to shed a tear in our presence throughout their lives without being told Big Boys Don't Cry.

There is a balance to be achieved between offering a sympathetic ear and being over-indulgent or making excuses where there has been bad behaviour. Martin Stephen is very critical of parents who believe their sons can do no wrong, something which is, he says, in his experience at school, a growing and damaging phenomenon. As a head teacher, he's always ready to listen to mitigating circumstances for misbehaviour, for instance if there are problems at home, but, with the responsibility of 1400 boys in his care, he has no time for parents who make feeble excuses for the way their sons have behaved or who refuse to co-operate with the school's disciplinary procedures.

As a parent, though, you have to weigh up all the possibilities. I would never make excuses for appalling behaviour, but would want to work with the staff at a school I trusted, like Manchester Grammar, to acknowledge and rectify a problem. But I had a harsh experience of this when Charlie was younger and at a different school. He was accused of bullying, which he told me about right away. I had difficulty believing that my son could be a bully, and told him so, but his reaction was to throw up his hands and confess all. We supported him in going to the headmaster and talked to him severely about how wrong it was to bully. At home, we punished him with withdrawal of privileges, while at school he suffered terribly from harsh punishments and humiliation. So much so, we eventually moved him and he began to flourish again.

It was a long time afterwards, in the car, when he suddenly said, 'It wasn't me you know'. When the whole story came out, it turned out that it had been another boy who'd done the bullying and Charlie had been his victim. The bully had been throwing Charlie's schoolbag into the mud and making his life a misery. This same boy had so intimidated the other children that, having decided that Charlie was going to be his target he had managed to persuade some of the younger ones to make a complaint against Charlie. He finally explained to me that he'd taken the rap, partly out of fear of this boy and partly because 'you just don't tell on people'. I had failed to take account of that schoolboy law of *omerta* and could probably have got to the truth much sooner if I had found a way of discussing the phenomenon with him, and reassured him that there are times when, if you've done nothing wrong and someone else has, it is OK at least to tell your parents. Then you can trust them to work out as a family the best way to progress.

Keeping the lines of communication open when children are very small is vitally important, because you never know what terrors or worries they are trying to live with until they tell you. I remember coming home from my days as a presenter on *Newsnight* once (we did very long shifts three or four days a week, from 10 a.m. sometimes to midnight) putting the key into the lock of a house in complete darkness, only to find the security chain was on inside. I threw pebbles at the bedroom window to no avail. My partner is an early riser who likes to be in bed by ten and sleeps like a dead man. I hissed through the letterbox, 'Will somebody please let me in?', when a ghostly little figure in red pyjamas appeared at the top of the stairs.

'Who's there?' Ed squeaked. He was all of three and shaking from top to toe. When he realised it was me he came down, stood on tiptoes, took the chain off and let me in. He sat on my lap in the sitting room for a while, sobbing and needing comfort, obviously afraid I was cross. (I was – I'd been outside in the freezing cold for half an hour – but tried not to show it, as he was so distressed.) Eventually I managed to ask him how the chain had come to be on, did Daddy forget I was out? No implied criticism of Ed, note. And it all came tumbling out.

He'd woken up after Daddy had gone to bed and felt frightened because he thought a burglar might come in. Forgetting that I was still out, he thought he'd make the house safe for everybody by putting the chain on. What made him think the house needed to be made safe for everybody? He'd been reading *Burglar Bill* at bedtime, so knew burglars came in at night-time when people were asleep. *Burglar Bill*, one of the most delightful children's books on the market, is about Burglar Bill and Burglar Betty who eventually give up their life of crime. I would never have imagined it could be a scary story, but it was.

It's difficult to know how to reassure boys that they can be safe at night, without resorting to keeping a gun or kitchen knife under the pillow. Charlie has suggested both solutions whenever the issue has come up. Children are exposed to various kinds of fears, initially in stories, and, as they get older, in newspapers, on radio and television. It's been especially difficult since September 11, as it is during any period of tension, as when the Iraqi War was looming. There are no hard and fast rules, but I've found that acknowledging and sharing the fear is more productive than dismissing it. In the case of the burglar, Ed and I discussed that even grown-ups can be frightened of being burgled, but we do our best to prevent it. So his putting the chain on was a positive thing, except it's always worth checking all the family are inside before you do it!

In the case of looming war or terrorism, there's no point in going further than they want you to go or piling on too much information if they are too young to take it in. Fergal Keene told me recently that his son, Daniel, at seven, had been watching *Newsround* and asked him, with a very worried look, whether we would be going to war with Iraq against Saddam Hussein? Fergal asked Daniel if he knew where Iraq was and what he knew about the Iraqi dictator. Daniel wasn't sure about any of it. Fergal managed to distract him from his anxiety by giving him a bit of a geography and history lesson and making him feel better informed.

Charlie managed to deflect his fears, at the age of four or five during the first Gulf War in 1991, by inventing the name, Sadman Hussein, but was often anxious as a small boy about my frequent trips into central London. His nervousness came to the surface when he warned me about walking near any rubbish bins. There had been a small IRA bomb in a bin near John Lewis in Oxford Street and he was terrified I would be caught up in such an atrocity. I promised him I would try not to walk past any rubbish bins and told him a little bit, in the simplest terms, about why the IRA are so cross with the British. It seemed to help.

September 11 was much less easy to explain. We'd all seen the dreadful images on television, but were unable to understand how such horror could happen. Ed was due to fly off to the States to begin his gap year just a few days later and, I have to say, the balance of reassurance had shifted. I asked him whether he was sure about going (I would have done anything to have prevented him getting on that plane) and he, with the glorious confidence of youth, told me nothing would happen and he wasn't going to let a few lunatics spoil the way he was going to live his life. He had a fantastic year and came home safely.

Another important reason for trusting and keeping lines of communication open is drugs. There's no doubt the government has sent out confused and muddled messages with the proposal to reclassify cannabis from Class 'B' to Class 'C' under the 1971 Misuse of Drugs Act. This would not mean, as most of the youngsters I've spoken to seem to think, legalisation of the drug – dealing and using in a public place would still involve penalties, although possession of small amounts for personal use would probably be overlooked.

The real danger, though, is the lack of information about the potential effects of cannabis. Those of us who may have confronted the occasional spliff in the '60s may well consider it to be far less harmful than tobacco or even alcohol, but there is strong new evidence that the stuff available on the streets nowadays is considerably more powerful than what was around twenty or thirty years ago. Research carried out recently in South London, where there is heavy use of the drug, has shown in the past ten years or so a significant rise in incidents of drug-induced psychosis caused by cannabis smoking; the rise being put down partly to the strength of the cannabis on sale and partly to a rise in frequent use. One of the researchers compared the increased level of use to that of an alcoholic, observing that the occasional joint at a party wouldn't do any harm, just as keeping within recommended alcohol levels is unlikely to be harmful, but smoking cannabis every day is as dangerous as drinking a bottle of vodka a day.

Martin and Jenny Stephen, again in their capacity as head teachers, are worried, particularly about early teenage boys between thirteen and fifteen. Acknowledging that these are the hardest years for boys, when hormones are pinging about and you're neither a boy nor a man, their concern is that the 'natural miseries of the age group' are compounded when a group begins to experiment with cannabis. In the group, which functions on secrecy and deception, depression, says Martin, can become contagious and any low self-esteem can be deepened. There is also, because of the underhand nature of the activity, a risk that the boys might suspend any moral code. Both Martin and Jenny are very strict in their response to cannabis use and deplore the 'middle-class culture change, which assumes they will take it'.

They have been astonished by parents who, having been called in to discuss individual boys whose mental state has become a cause for concern, have shown surprise that depressive mood changes and a sudden deterioration in school work might be brought about by cannabis use. They advise that parents look out for the signs (often difficult to spot when behaviour during this period can be volatile): mood changes and deterioration in work, accompanied by giddiness, excessive hunger for sweet things (the munchies), glassy eyes with extended pupils and bizarre behaviour, such as taking the dog out late at night in the middle of November with a group of friends (generally boys don't do such altruistic things in the freezing cold unless they are up to no good!).

If you discover a boy is using, Martin recommends putting aside the temptation to go along with the current fashion for parents to be friends and not to be nasty. The problem needs tough handling, he says, because the stakes are too high. He has seen a number of boys lose the plot completely as a result of parents either failing to recognise what's going on or being too 'liberal' about it.

Personally, I've always spoken to the boys about the dangers of drugs, alcohol and cigarettes. Smoking tobacco is something they've always disapproved of, having seen the struggles I have had with nicotine addiction and they have taken seriously the anti-smoking propaganda they've received at school in biology lessons. Alcohol is much more a part of the laddish culture that seems to prevail these days and causes so much anxiety to parents – although they do seem to be less cavalier than my generation was about drinking and driving. But they need to know the facts about booze: that it kills more Britons than heroin, opium, Ecstasy, crack and methadone put together; that half of all incidents of domestic violence are fuelled by drink, as are town and city centre fights; and that those who don't end up with a knife in the chest may drive their cars home only to despatch a few more to the morgue along the way.

We have never been puritanical about drink or soft drugs, merely pointing out the risks; discussing how easy or otherwise it might be to say 'No', when a joint is passed around at a party; talking about what pleasure there might be in losing your inhibitions among friends; and always reassuring the boys that they can talk to us without fear about any concerns they might have. They've had the occasional glass of wine or beer with us at home. I have told them I'm not prepared to have cannabis smoking on the premises because of concerns about the legal questions and would prefer they didn't smoke it at all because of the health issues. This was especially relevant for Ed, as he recognised that he had to achieve top A level grades to pursue his ambition to be a vet, so risking brain or memory damage was not an option; it was equally relevant for Charlie because he needs to be at the peak of physical fitness to stay on top in rugby. I've pointed out that they have enough information to make their own decisions and, as teenagers, I have to trust their judgement.

Boys are bound to get drunk occasionally – post-exam times are the most dangerous, as the Blairs discovered when Euan passed out in Leicester Square. My two have always laughed at me for my lessons in what to do if a pal passes out – lie him on his side and watch him, he could drown in his own vomit – and accuse me of being over-cautious, but I like to think that they wouldn't leave a mate in the state that Euan was abandoned that night. Ed certainly seems to have got the message and whilst he enjoys going out for a drink, was shocked at the tone of the Students' Union material sent out when he was about to go up to university. At nineteen, he recognised the dangers of leaflets that promoted seeing 'who can drink who under the table in Freshers' Week', and was appalled at the implication that a lad can only enjoy himself if he's getting blind drunk.

Little boys love a cuddle and some of the most pleasurable times of my life have been spent curled up together with my sons on the sofa or the bed in the evening (bunk beds are not conducive, as I discovered to my cost, unless you're prepared to climb up the ladder on alternate nights to make sure you're sharing yourself equally). A freshly bathed small boy has a sweet scent unlike any other and a little sleepy, tousle-haired moppet arriving at five in the morning for a family cuddle may be a bit of a pain, but snuggling down together for another hour or so is comforting for everyone and usually buys another couple of hours sleep.

We took our boys into bed with us from when they were very tiny. They had a cot in our room until they were a couple of months old, and if they woke up in the middle of the night for a feed I would simply bring them into bed, feed them and we would all fall asleep together. They both settled well to moving into their own room as they began to sleep though the night, but all hell broke loose at about one year old: they were both big and strong, even at this age and, long before they were able to walk, managed to somersault over the bars of the cot, land with a thud and crawl along the landing to our room, scramble up the side of the bed and snuggle down between us. This carried on until they were both around three or four and eventually led to David setting himself up in a spare room and we have, very comfortably I should add, and with mutual agreement, had our own rooms ever since.

My theory about why the boys did this concerns my being a full-time working mother. The middle of the night was the one time they knew I was their captive and available for close physical contact. Happily it never worried us as parents, but it is something to consider if you are in similar circumstances. It wouldn't work out for every family. There are also some people who now express concern about sleeping with babies and there does seem to be some evidence that some babies have suffocated as a result. Both mine came through unscathed and there was never a question of us not waking up if they wriggled or showed any signs of distress. I would certainly not recommend it if you've been drinking or have taken any drugs.

Like my boys, India Knight's sons are thriving in a naturally physically demonstrative family:

'I am the same with the boys and they with me, for the time being at least. They love being kissed and stroked, although obviously, the nibbly kisses on the freshly bathed bottom stopped some time ago.

Oscar, who's ten, still loves being kissed, even in front of his friends (on the rare occasions when I manage to collect him from school). Archie, seven, is like a cat and practically purrs with delight when you cuddle him. I think the trick is not to do interrupty kissing/cuddling, which is irritating even if you're an adult. But general lying about the sofa having backrubs cuddling works very well. They've always been kissed and they've always kissed me, so I don't anticipate much change. Obviously I adjust my kissing urges to the situation, and I don't expect I'll be squidging teenagers and sniffing their hair in transports of delight, but I don't see why the physical closeness should stop.'

The poet and novelist Jackie Kay has found that, even with her teenage son, physical closeness hasn't had to stop.

'My boy is very affectionate, even though he is a big 6 foot teenager. He is still a sucker for a cuddle and is happy giving other people hugs "Hello" and "Goodbye". I imagine he'll always be comfortable with that if he is now. He's also a boy who cries and has always been a boy who cries a lot. I do find that even feminists and thinkers still fall into this trap of putting the sexes into clearly defined categories, boys are like this and girls are like this, so there isn't a lot of room. I think these notions of differences between the sexes are even more extreme than they were in the more liberal '60s and '70s. It is obviously quite different being a man or boy from being a woman or girl, but not necessarily in the ways we've been taught to think, i.e. strong/weak. I think men are weak actually, much weaker than women and less emotionally independent. Wee boys are more clingy to their mums than wee girls and somewhere along the line the whole picture gets changed. 'How' is the interesting question.'

The research evidence suggests that Jackie may be right in describing boys as the weaker sex. In March 2002, Dr Sebastian Kraemer, consultant child and adolescent psychiatrist at the Tavistock Clinic in London wrote in the *British Medical Journal* about what he calls boys' biological inferiority. Dr Kraemer claims that their frailty becomes evident from the moment of conception. He says studies have indicated that stresses in a pregnant woman are more likely to affect male embryos, which are more commonly subject to brain damage, cerebral palsy and stillbirth. A newborn girl is said to be the physiological equivalent of a four- to six-week-old boy. Kraemer also says that these differences manifest themselves throughout life. Boys are three times more susceptible to developmental disorders, such as autism, hyperactivity and stammering; as they reach adolescence, they are at much greater risk of making dangerous experiments with drugs and alcohol; and they are several times more likely to kill themselves than are women. Seventy-five per cent of suicides in the UK are by males; suicides by young men, aged fifteen to twenty-four are now rising – in 2003, 67 per cent higher than in 1982 (figures from the mental health charity MIND). Dr Kraemer puts boys' inferiority down to evolution:

> 'In evolutionary terms, men are redundant. It doesn't matter if there are a lot of damaged males around as long as there are brilliant ones who get to the top in the primitive pecking order. We don't need many males because you only need a few to reproduce the species.'

I am not altogether convinced by the biological/evolutionary argument, even though Kraemer argues that the differences can be seen even in the early months before boys start to cover up their emotional sensitivity. He cites experiments with boy-girl twins – like Richard Denton's – where the boy seems to get very upset when his sister cries, whereas she barely bats an eyelid if he cries. But we saw in the first chapter how the difference in the way we treat boys and girls begins in the delivery room, so, perhaps, if baby boys and toddlers do seem to be more demanding, with higher energy and emotional swings, it could be that, from birth onwards, girls are simply getting more sympathetic solicitude, whereas boys, being deprived, need to find other ways of attracting attention.

Whether Kraemer is right or not about what he calls a biological flaw in boys, we are agreed about what needs to be done. He urges parents to resist the conditioning, which suggests boys don't need so much physical affection, and to give their sons the attention they crave. He says this is especially important in the first four years when most of the brain development takes place.

> 'If boys are properly cared for they won't have so many develop-mental problems. For parents the object is to produce courageous men. A real man is a man who has the capacity to know his strengths and weaknesses and doesn't need protective armour.'

This advice is especially important at those difficult times when boys try to assert themselves and break away from Mum's clutches. It's again very helpful at these times if fathers are involved because then boys won't see nurture as something that only women do. But if mums are solely responsible for picking up and dropping off from school, and doing all the care in the home, boys might feel that the only way to become independent is to reject the 'female'. If dads are around as well, this gender difficulty is less likely to arise.

If Mum is the only person involved, the first sign of this problem seems to show at the time of potty-training. Angela Phillips notes in her book, *The Trouble with Boys*:

> 'Right at the beginning, at the tender age of two, whilst the girls see the introduction of a potty as a way to be grown up – to be more like Mummy – the boy is likely to perceive it as a way to control him, to take something away from him. Of course, both girls and boys may have problems and may regress under stress to a baby stage in which the world seemed a more benign place and they felt less responsible for their actions, but it is boys who are four to five times more likely to visit clinics for help in controlling this basic bodily function. Perhaps they need the involvement of another adult to take control from the hands of the mothers and put it where it rightly belongs.'

I have to say, we never had any problems with potty-training but we did have the live-in help of Jeanne, our properly trained nanny, who never became anxious about anything, as far as I recall. She had the potty around from about the age of a year and if they wanted to use it, they did; if not, she wasn't too fussed. We were both involved in nappy changing and going to the loo as well, so it was never allowed to become an issue.

What was much harder was leaving them to go to work. There were no problems at all until they were each about eighteen months old, and I don't recall Charlie creating quite as much mayhem as Ed did. Second boys do seem to be much more confident generally than first-borns – no doubt picking up on the parents' greater confidence and seeing that older brothers go away and come back or get left behind without suffering any permanent loss or damage. But Ed used to clutch at my skirts and scream, 'Please don't go, Mummy'. I would spend ages comforting, hugging and reassuring him, until finally I would have to drag myself away, weeping all the way to the office. Jeanne would invariably report that he would turn to her with a grin the moment the door closed and say, 'Right, what shall we do now then?' I suspect I suffered more than he did and he never did it to his dad! From an early age children can spot a sucker!

Some of the parents I've spoken to have been terribly worried about how clingy their boys can become when it's time to go to nursery or school. Some psychologists do say that boys suffer worse from the separation than girls, probably because they have already picked up on the fact that they are supposed to be brave about it, whereas girls will have had much more open support in making the transition from home to school. For us, playschool was a good way of making the move. It's rarely of any help to full-time working parents who need childcare all day, as it's generally only open for half a day for a couple of hours. But, as parents or carers are encouraged to stay with the children at least one day a week, playschool can be a helpful interim measure. We found it a useful means for one of the three of us to be around whilst the boys got used to negotiating their way around other children and gradually being left over a period of months.

Jackie Kay is lucky to have a son who doesn't balk at physical contact when he's a teenager. India Knight was horrified at my suggestion that her two might, at some point, back off. But, generally speaking, they do. The first break seems to happen at about six or seven, when they really don't want to hold your hand in public anymore and react to a kiss outside the school gate with the same revulsion that they'd show if they'd bitten into a poison apple, but they're still up for snuggles and cuddles at home. Then there's a steady withdrawal at around twelve or thirteen, around the time the door slamming and grunting begin.

It can, actually, be a bit of a relief, especially if you have two or more of them. I did find it a little wearing when the kind of sibling rivalry that once led Ed to yell at Charlie in the back of the car, 'Stop looking out of my window!', developed into scraps and squabbles about who was going to sit next to me on the sofa. I'd end up like the ham in the sandwich, an arm around each of them, whilst they surreptitiously pinched and prodded each other in the hope that one would give up in disgust.

It can be hurtful, though, when one's partly flown the nest, the other is raging through adolescence and there's no-one to fight over you any more. Charlie – operating in a totally secure family background – shocked me recently by expressing his fury at my being 'too affectionate' and telling him I loved him too many times a day. I've backed off a bit since, and certainly wouldn't put my arms around him or expect to kiss, hug or even touch him in public. But I won't stop telling him I love him or waiting for those opportunities when he is ready for a cuddle.

As India says, it's unfair to press physical contact on them, but it is vital, though, during this awkward period, to look out for subtle signs of a craving for affection. I find adolescent boys frequently develop pains in the back and neck, needing a massage at bedtime or when we're flopped out in front of the TV. I have a theory that the reason men are seemingly so beset by aches and pains and cope so much worse with illness than women is because being ill or hurting is an acceptable way for them to ask for a spot of nurture without being seen as soft.

I much prefer giving Charlie a back rub to enduring his other invitation for a cuddle. It's usually when I'm in my bedroom, getting ready to go out. He waits till he knows I'm likely to have done my hair, put on my make-up and got dressed (anything less would be just too disgusting for words!), then he flies into the room and rugby tackles me onto the bed. I go along with it – and he hasn't broken any of my bones – yet.

It does get better as they get older and break away from home. One of my greatest pleasures nowadays is to take Ed out for a meal in the evening, chat about the good and the awful times we've had together and forgive each other for any real hurt or offence we may have caused. All that hard work in keeping the lines of communication open paid off in the end. He even hugs and kisses me at the end of the evening – in the street!

I have another theory, which may be of comfort to those of you who are going through the worst of teenage times just now. The more horrible your boy is, the greater the compliment to your skills as a parent. If they didn't trust in your love completely they would never dare to be so vile and, if they didn't go through a period of being so unspeakable, you would never, ever be able to let them go.

CHAPTER FOUR

GIRLS! YUK!

For this chapter there'll be, on the whole, no names and no pack drill, as it seems to me grossly unfair to ask parents to talk about grappling with their sons' blossoming sexuality whilst revealing the identity of those sons. Parents have talked openly to me about their struggles with what to tell their sons when; how to distinguish perfectly normal 'I'll show you mine, if you'll show me yours' scenarios from potentially abusive situations; what to say about pornography and pictures of *Loaded* and *FHM*'s scantily dressed young women appearing on the bedroom wall; whether to ignore stained sheets or try to prevent masturbation; when to concede it's OK for a girlfriend to stay overnight or how to help a boy who thinks he prefers other boys to girls.

The greatest anxiety for the parents I've spoken to is how to teach our boys that sex can be glorious and not at all dirty, whilst also giving them a sense of responsibility for the feelings of partners, and wisdom and maturity with regard to pregnancy, sexually transmitted disease, rape and sexual abuse. We're all aware that our boys are exposed to ambiguous and wildly conflicting messages about sex from a variety of sources. Films, television and other forms of popular culture, particularly the 'lads' mags', seem to trumpet an 'always-up-for-it culture', but never appear to address the possible pitfalls of getting involved in a sexual relationship. Schools and churches tend to promote a Just-Say-No culture, which is idealistic, but for most young people, unrealistic. So I'll examine the latest and most sensible research and pass on the experiences and advice of other mums and dads, but change names where necessary, if that's OK.

The 'girls-are-yuk!' stage seems to start at around six and last till twelve or thirteen, coinciding, of course, with the two big hormonal rushes boys have to cope with. India Knight still puzzles over her boys' propensity to feign throwing up whenever a girl is mentioned: 'They invariably display utter horror. I say, but I'm a girl and so are X, Y and Z whom you love – all relatives. This apparently is "different"!' By thirteen or fourteen, girls are beginning to appear much less yukky, but still seem to be perceived as alien territory, even among boys who have sisters, or female friends at a co-educational school.

Don't get anxious, by the way, if by sixteen or seventeen, your son seems to take no interest in girls at all, but appears to be perfectly happy with his lot and expresses no concerns about his sexuality. One of the parents I spoke to, Cathy, tells me: 'At sixteen, he seems to think girls are boring and that he could have four girl-friends at the snap of his fingers, but doesn't want to yet, because he'd have to hang around with them in his lunch hour. He seems to think girls are a different species still and doesn't get them.'

What is of concern is the kind of conversation I heard around my kitchen table a couple of years ago. A group of then thirteen-year-olds had been to a party the night before and were discussing their experiences over breakfast. In this particular sample of half a dozen lads, John had been going out with Jane for a year. She wouldn't even snog him! Cor! They all agreed, she must be frigid. Another girl was described as easy; a third was a right slag. It was obvious from ten minutes' eavesdropping that girl power is still something of a fantasy. Whichever way the girl jumps, she's damned. Not much different from when I was at school.

A lot of boys' conversations about sex at this age are naturally based on bravado and are notoriously unreliable as a record of what they have actually been up to. It's their attitudes that need to be addressed and we should be getting extremely anxious about the kind of views expressed in research carried out in 1999 by the Zero Tolerance Charitable Trust in Glasgow. Males aged between four-teen and twenty-four were asked whether they thought sexual violence against women was justified. One in ten said they would rape a woman if they thought no one would find out. One in eight said, 'Yes', if the girl had slept with loads of people. One in six believed it was OK to force sex on a woman if you were married to her. Six per cent said they would be happy to ignore a girl saying 'No', if the boy had spent a lot of money on a night out.

Just as boys have suffered a dearth of advice about their emotions, appearance and health, so too they've been left floundering when sex rears his head, which perhaps explains why they are so wary and ignorant of girls as fellow human beings who are also struggling to find a mature sexual identity. Parents find it the hardest topic to be open about and, historically, there's been little published information aimed at boys that might be helpful.

In the mid-nineteenth-century *Penny Dreadful* stories for boys, women were described as 'daughters of poverty who would sell their virtue for a loaf of bread', or as 'dangerous temptresses', reminiscent of the wicked queen in H. Rider Haggard's *She*, or 'evil hags' whose love of the demon drink would drag a boy into the gates of hell. Edwin Brett's *The Darling of our Crew*, written in 1880 is typical of the genre:

> 'She made her way to a keg which stood before the fire. From this she took a pint of raw brandy . . . chuckling fiendishly . . . she drank half of it at a draught. Now madness glared in her eyes unmistakeably. She drank off the remainder of the fearful potion and danced . . . She stretched forth her long talons . . . as she advanced to where Jack was, shrieking, "Now, boy, you shall be my victim. Ha! Ha! Ha!'

Scary stuff!

Professor Jeffrey Weeks, in his book *Sex Politics and Society – the Regulation of Sex since 1800* finds precious little by way of 'sex education' for boys and young men apart from dire warnings about the dangers of masturbation:

> 'By the mid-nineteenth century the focus of interest in the treatises against masturbation was more clearly young people than adults, and there seems little doubt this was connected with the re-definitions of

adolescence. For pre-industrial society, youth was a long transition period lasting from the first signs of independence of the young child to marriage.

Adolescence was now seen as a special stage of life and one that was, moreover, clearly differentiated on class lines. The real crucible for the age group's social and psychological qualities was the elite secondary school, associated in particular with the rise of a more extensive education. The result for the middle-class child was an increased state of dependence, longer than that experienced by the previous generation. There were also other changes, such as available reading matter. In 1855 Boy's Own Magazine *appeared, followed by* Boy's Own Paper *and* Boy's Penny Magazine, *addressed to a new class of boys, and which signalled significant shifts in public attitudes, particularly acting to increase sex segregation and reinforce stereotypes.'*

Weeks points to the doctors who developed theories of masturbatory insanity: 'characterised by intense self-regard and conceit . . . failure of intelligence, nocturnal hallucinations and suicidal and homicidal propensities'. Baden Powell, the founder of the Scout movement believed that masturbation checks the semen from getting its full chance of making a strong, manly man, 'You are throwing away the seed that has been handed down to you as a trust instead of keeping it and ripening it for bringing a son to you later on.'

Weeks discusses the popularity of physical sanctions to prevent masturbation,

'including the development of elaborate machines which sensitively responded to erections or physically prevented masturbation. More important probably was the guilt induced by the constant strictures, which made the struggle against one's wicked urges a constant effort of will.'

We've already seen, in Chapter Three, how ideas about boys' sexual development were reflected in the magazines of the time and in the inducements to 'take a cold bath', but as Weeks points out, attitudes took a long time to change. By 1895 *'there was a greater emphasis on masturbation as a symptom rather than as a cause. Masturbation did not become respectable, but there was a new stress on its ability to rob adolescence of real fulfilment, and this was even echoed in the work of sex reformers, such as Havelock Ellis, and expressed in G. Stanley Hall's two volumes on adolescence.*

But, despite this slight shift in the taboos, as late as the 1920s Havelock Ellis and Albert Moll were still able to recommend little metal suits of armour fitted over the genitals and attached to a locked belt as a prophylaxis for masturbation, and sex education books continued to inveigh against the solitary vice well into the second half of the twentieth century. Pre-adult sexuality remained something to be organised and controlled.'

The headmaster of Eton in 1913, the Reverend Edward Littleton, summed up the duties of parents and teachers with regard to boys and control of their sexuality thus:

'Those who are working and hoping, however feebly, to encompass the lives of boys and girls with wholesome atmosphere must know that in regard to sexuality two factors stand out. First, that in proportion as the adolescent mind gets absorbed in sex questions, wreckage of life ensues. Secondly, that sanity and upright manliness are destroyed, not only by the reading of obscene stuff, but by a premature interest in sex matters, however it be excited.'

By 1925 *The Life Saving Scout and Guard* magazine, closely related to the Scout movement, was dishing up some pretty sniffy exhortations which, were they not so sadly misogynist in tone, would be hilarious. In October of that year a scout had asked whether it was proper to continue his weekly trips to the dance hall. He obviously enjoyed them, but had been warned he shouldn't go. What did the editor think?

'To begin with there is nothing very constructive about dancing, to a Scout or Guard who has other opportunities for physical exercise. The attraction is a social one. Young folk like the lights, the music,

the dresses and the chatter. The conversation is not on a high level of intelligence. If a boy goes to meet girlfriends it is scarcely likely that the best sort of girls will be found. If he goes to meet boy-friends, the chances of meeting decent, manly fellows is much less in the dance hall than at outdoor games.

Dance hall conditions, generally speaking are . . . stale air, late hours and dances that are often questionable in their moral influ-ence. We can dismiss the talk of "poetry in motion". We would suggest that our questioner and all others interested should sit down and calmly discover why they like the dance hall. Do you like dressing up for it? Do you like the cross talk or the music? Or what is it you actually do like?

When you have done that, measure up the reason why you like the dance with your Scout and Guard Pledge and Declaration. Be honest about it. If it doesn't tally, do the job that every fellow with anything in them has to do. Cut out the lowest and stick to the highest. We stand for mastery over all habits. The thing we feel we cannot do without, we cut out, just to show who is boss of the establishment. Nearly all the fellows we know who are keen on Scouting and manly things and had a contempt for the dance hall have found the right girl somehow. The dance hall sort may be good partners for a hop across the floor, but they are rarely much good as partners on the lifelong trail.'

It's not too difficult to read the message between the lines – only loose girls go dancing; dancing's about sex; sexual arousal is to be avoided at all costs; go for a run and take a cold bath! No fun, no muddle, just *Mens Sana in Corpore Sano* and the suggestion that a boy's aim in life is to seek out not love, affection and sexual compatibility, but a suitable wife to keep the home fires burning whilst the boy goes out and does 'manly' things. Heather Formaini, in her 1990 book, *Men*, found very little had changed:

'The method by which a man chooses a wife, the female counter-part, is very often more in keeping with the conventions of his back-ground and his culture than with his real feelings. His choice of partner will be made on the basis of class, ethnicity, geography,

personal appearance and religion. If, for emotional reasons, he entertains the idea of marrying a woman outside his class, his culture or his economic group, he is very likely to be dissuaded from seeing her as a possible life companion. It would be much more likely that he would be encouraged by his family and peers to have some sort of "informal" relationship with her, but to marry someone more like himself. This is the way traditions are upheld and this is also the way that other structures which underpin masculinity are kept in place: class, religion, race, economics and so on. Feelings will come a long way down the list.'

Accounting, no doubt, in some respects, for the failure in modern society of so many marriages where the commitment may not have been freely given. A jolly good pointer to parents that, whilst we may want our sons- and daughters-in-law to be just like us, it may not be the best way to ensure a happy home life for our grand-children (more on this in Chapter Eight).

The fun end of the market for boys' reading in the period after the First World War was dominated by D. C. Thompson, the Dundee publisher that produced the *Adventure*, the *Rover*, the *Wizard*, the *Hotspur* and the *Skipper*, which are described in E. S. Turner's analysis of boys' popular reading, *Boys Will Be Boys*, published in 1947, as:

'A curious mixture of inhibitions and lack of inhibitions. The problem of sex was very simply solved: girls did not exist. Occasionally, but very occasionally, there may be a reference to some fellow's sister being rescued from a fire, but it could just as easily have been a tame goat or a sack of flour. This ban on females was probably the most absolute in the history of boys' magazines. The existence of an opposite sex was admitted only in the adver-tisements of magazines which catered for a fellow's sister: "Famous Perfumes Free – this week Phul Nana – with every copy of the great new story paper The Mascot magazine".'

The magazines that are most likely to be read by young teenage boys in the twenty-first century are *FHM* and *Loaded*, guaranteed to send any woman who has, as I have, devoted her life to drawing up peace treaties in the battle of the sexes, into a flat spin of disappointment. Jo Elvin, editor of *Glamour*, and the launch editor of the girls' teen magazine *Sugar* shares my irritation at the way in which these magazines play into the worst aspects of traditional, ogling male sexuality and at the way they demean and potentially damage women.

She argues that the launch of such magazines in the early nineties had a profoundly damaging effect on the progress which had been made by the women's movement in criticising the portrayal of women as available objects made for men's titillation. The new teen magazines became part of a bruising backlash, which ridiculed any woman, like Clare Short, who had campaigned against Page 3 in parliament, who dared to stick her head above the parapet and complain. We (as I count myself among such campaigners) were invariably portrayed as a pretty humourless lot with no sense of what was ludicrously dubbed 'post-feminist irony'. As Jo Elvin told me:

> '*For me it started with the lads' mags. I was astonished at the number of young starlets who were prepared to pose for the cover of* FHM *in her bra and pants, pouting out the message, "I love sex, me". It pandered to a lad culture which forced young women to embrace the "ironic". Anything that was passed off as a joke was OK. The girls had to be laddettes – hard drinking, up for it any time, anywhere – and they were meant to find Anna Friel taking her kit off hilarious.*'

In defence of the lads' magazines, they were, when they began, quite fun; and there was, within the pages of both *FHM* and *Loaded*, some attempt to address the concerns of young men about their sex lives in a sympathetic and witty way. Some of the writing was first rate. They have, I'm afraid, deteriorated and now seem to appeal to the lowest form of witless misogyny. A quick spin through the most recent issues showed, in one edition of *FHM*: Sex Mad: The Girls Who Can't Say No, Jenna's Sex Lessons: Got a Disgracefully Filthy Sex Query? Send it to Jenna; Ladies' Confessions – Your Other Halves Put Jenna to Shame; Girls on the

Sofa – all Sorts of Smutty Stuff and Christina Aguilera – Musicdom's Sauciest Minx on Girl Fighting, Masturbation and that Spat with Kelly Osbourne.' *Loaded* offered: 'Shag Academy, How to Charm Posh Birds into Bed; Sauna Girls and Five Up and Coming TV Babes who Aim to Ensnare Men with their Pert Bums and Stuff.' It's pornography posing as innocent entertainment.

Teenage girls have fared a little better. There was a blip in the mid-twentieth century when girls' and women's magazines rather overemphasised how to get and please your man in the permissive hey day of *Cosmopolitan*, but more recently, in 2002, the editors of teen magazines were praised by the Government's teenage pregnancy unit (charged with lowering the rate of teenage pregnancy and preventing drug and alcohol abuse), for their ability to raise awareness in an informative way without being patronising. But, even today, as in the past, it tends to be the girls who're perceived as the guardians of their own purity and the first line of defence against rampantly dangerous male sexuality. The boys are invariably the villains of the piece. An extract from *Things We Must Tell Our Girls*, a publication for 'Working Mothers' published in 1901 would hardly seem out of place today.

> '*We cannot speak too plainly about romping or flirting, the walking about after dark with men and boys which is common in most places. A girl should know why familiarities and rough romping, and jostling and hustling and late walks at night might lead to harm and not merely think of it as something of which her mother disapproves. There is the wrong of it towards the man . . . how it is cruel to encourage him to be familiar and to play at lovemaking or "flirt" as it is sometimes called . . . the girl has a right to know what familiar caresses with men may cost her. Tell her of how the man goes Scot free if he gets the girl into trouble and that it is she who must bear the months of suspense and dread, the pain and weariness, the disgrace in the eyes of friends and finally the agony and shame when the baby comes.*'

No-one, and it's still the case, has ever thought it possible or necessary to make an attractive and interesting magazine for teenage boys which would help them develop a pride in and a sense of responsibility for their own sexual behaviour. No wonder boys for so many generations have believed sex was dirty and dangerous and have so deeply resented, feared and ridiculed the girls and women who, while arousing, while their physical interest, were trained to repel it at all costs.

Boys do, of course, get sex education at school, which is largely supported by parents. Consistently between 94 and 96 per cent of parents believe schools should provide education about sex and personal relationships and there is considerable academic evidence to show that a liberal sex education has positive effects on knowledge, attitudes and behaviour. But there is also evidence showing that boys frequently reject the lessons altogether, either by not turning up, or by disrupting them with bravado. Simon Forrest of the Department of Sexually Transmitted Diseases at University College London, in his paper 'Big and Tough: Boys Learning about Sexuality and Manhood', argues that the sex education on offer fails to address boys' needs, so we should create an environment in which boys can reject the pressure to behave in 'rigid sex-stereotypical ways'.

Forrest includes in his paper a study, carried out in 1998, of

> science text books which showed 'much sexism, usually taking the form of an assumption of heterosexuality and sex equating only with penetrative vaginal intercourse, within which women are mostly portrayed as "passive, supine receptacles into which sperm are deposited". Much more time is devoted to describing sexual intercourse from the point of view of the male rather than the female and female orgasm was mentioned in only five of the fifteen books reviewed. Bodies are always shown with the male penetrating, lying on top of the female'.

Forrest describes a visit to a secondary school where staff were evaluating their sex education programme for thirteen and fourteen year olds:

> 'After the lesson, the teacher said he felt frustration . . . these boys,

he said, got nothing out of the sex education. They could not engage with it. They were just immature. I asked what the girls thought of them. He said they liked them, for being funny and challenging, but they thought they were immature too. He pointed out some work the girls had done in a single sex group. I copied out the words from the sheets pinned to the wall:

WHY BOYS LIE ABOUT SEX
To impress their partner
Insecure about their ability
To hide the fact they are gay
Because they think their friends have all had sex
To make girls want to have sex with them – it makes them look
  experienced
To feel grown up
To impress their friends
Because their girlfriend has had sex
Look hard
Feel the need to lose their virginity
So they're not called names, e.g. frigid/bent
Make them seem mature

School sex education often seems to exacerbate the tensions between girls and boys. Work like that of the girls presented above is highly likely to antagonise boys, regardless of whether it adequately reflects what they say or believe. Consequently, discussions can collapse into arguments in which girls and boys line up against each other. Girls will call boys immature. Boys will accuse girls of trying to annoy them.'

It's also apparent that this kind of atmosphere can be hurtful and damaging to young gays and lesbians – partly because any discussion of homosexuality is now seen as 'dangerous territory' for schools (ever since the Conservative government introduced clause 28, banning its 'promotion'), but also because boys obviously feel discouraged and doubtful, judging by the way the classes are run, that the issues will be explored in a sympathetic manner. Rather they build on what they with their peers see as 'acceptable' masculinity by knocking what they hope they are not – gay. The Stonewall survey, 'Queer bashing', described how much homophobic bullying goes on in schools. Ninety percent had been called names, 61 per cent harassed, 48 per cent violently attacked and 22 per cent 'beaten up'. Of the violent attacks, 40 per cent had taken place in schools and 79 per cent of name-calling had been by fellow students.

The justification of sex education, as required by the current government, seems to be the prevention of teenage pregnancies in line with the old pattern portraying girls as 'at risk', inactive and unwilling participants in any sexual encounter, and boys as dangerous missiles, with no concept of self-control, out to plant their sperm in any unsuspecting female. The nonsensical idea that girls are good and boys are bad, encountered earlier on, seems to pervade the atmosphere yet again at adolescence. Boys criticised the sex education they received in a Health Education Authority report in 1999, saying they found the censorious atmosphere unhelpful:

> 'Normally we are told things that other people think are important.
> It concentrates too much on women and periods.
> It's mostly negative, don't do this or this will happen.'

This is obviously not an environment conducive to talking about sex seriously or giving boys the opportunity to express the worries that research shows they will voice in a safe environment. Interestingly, both boys and girls, when asked to describe the major motivations for their first sexual intercourse, rated the three highest as being in love, curiosity and being the natural outcome of a relationship; the girls rating love first and the boys putting it third.

Forrest concludes that boys are still dominated by the pressures they are put under, not by teachers or by girls, but by other males. Thus they portray sexual experience, particularly loss of virginity, as an achievement:

> 'this pursuit of sexual excellence in men produces a raft of concerns that can undermine their ability to form intimate emotional bonds.

*They can end up preoccupied with penis size, maintaining an erec-
tion, making sexual intercourse last a long time and achieving
simultaneous orgasms. The perceived focus on pregnancy and
women's sexual health is not felt to be relevant by most boys . . .
Boys often enter into problematic and challenging behaviour in sex
education lessons while concealing profound concerns about sex
and sexuality. The behaviour of boys in sex education classes can
be seen as an attempt to distance themselves from showing feelings,
which may put them at a disadvantage with their male peers.*

*The importance to boys of using knowledge, experiences and
prejudices about sexuality to gain status within their male peer
groups is evident . . . we ought to acknowledge that talking about
sexuality and gender with men implies addressing their experience
of relationships with other men in male peer groups as much as
their experience of sexual relationships with individual women or
men. There must be scope for dealing positively with male anxiety
about sexual performance and showing that there is something
enriching to be had from engaging in sex as part of emotional
relationships.'*

Forrest doesn't give any guidance as to how sex education lessons
could be better run to address these difficulties for boys, but when
I read his work, so much fell into place. The pictures culled from
FHM and *Loaded* which appeared on the bedroom wall were not
necessarily for titillation or designed to infuriate Mum, but were
there to impress male friends. Evidence on the computer that porn
sites had been visited, or detailed phone bills that revealed calls to
'mucky' numbers demonstrated a joint male activity, which had
always occurred when male friends had been round.

There are important lessons here for schools. Sex education as
it's currently formulated is not helpful if it doesn't bring the boys
along with it. Governments who pronounce on these matters will
not easily get it right, as there are so many potential religious and
social minefields to confront. It is possible to offend all of the
people for most of the time. The last time, for instance, that
marriage came up for discussion, in March 2000, it was agreed with
the Bishops that it would be promoted as of key importance to

family life and the raising of children. Inevitably, the happily unmarried, but committed, and struggling single parents were furious; but, equally, Conservative peers were steaming at the suggestion that stable relationships, possibly even gay ones, would be put on an equal footing with marriage.

Let me offer an honourable alternative. At school under the heading Biology, we could confine reproduction, the possible transmission of disease and the technical means of preventing both to the cool, clinical environment of the science laboratory (employing, of course, those few science text books that have been found to give a more rounded picture of female sexuality than lying back in the missionary position and thinking of England!). All the other difficult questions surrounding human sexuality: marriage, cohabitation, responsibility, social impact and what we mean by masculinity and femininity could be taught under the banner of a new school discipline: Gender Studies.

The late Professor Sue Lees of the University of North London pointed out in her 2000 paper 'Gender, Education and Citizenship' that the kind of power relations between the sexes described in the Zero Tolerance Research and present in the conversation I heard around my dinner table (see page 87) are rarely, if ever, discussed in schools and consequently never change. Girls, she found, often say they'll get married to avoid 'being left on the shelf', but see it as a negative lifestyle choice. It's a means of getting sexual respectability, but, because most of the domestic tasks are still performed by women, even if they go out to work, they see it as a restriction on their chances of becoming full and active citizens. One girl told her: 'I'll get married when I've had my life' – it's that idea, again, of girls and women not wanting to be lumbered with a man who behaves like one of his children.

We're doing our boys a terrible disservice if education gives them the impression that sex is only about performance and fails to set it into the context of sexual politics. The term, Gender Studies, would take the smutty, giddy, competitive edge out of sex education and give schools the chance to discuss in a much broader context the important political issues of the past fifty years or so as they have influenced personal and family life.

Gender Studies should include just for starters the history of relations between men and women in the nineteenth and twentieth centuries, the extent to which women were disadvantaged in education and work and why it was necessary for policies to change, how boys and men influence each other, how attitudes to abortion, rape and homosexuality have changed and why. It should teach young people what the law now requires of them, of the arguments about pornography and the portrayal of both men and women in porn and advertising. They should certainly be made aware of the introduction of the Child Support Agency in the early nineties, and the political discussions about men, reproduction and responsibility, both financial and emotional, for children, whether planned or not.

It's my view that, whilst in current sex education classes, which seem to focus on female issues and the prevention of pregnancy, boys may well switch off; by contrast, a much more intelligent and appealing approach would be to tackle the subject from a position where 'the personal is political', something that concerns not only girls, but also boys and their futures. The fact that five minutes' unprotected knee trembling behind the bike sheds might cost £400 a month in maintenance payments might act as a much more powerful contraceptive than a moral lecture which serves only to annoy and embarrass.

Such an approach would offer boys the first opportunity to be exposed to their own history and their place in the most influential movement of modern times – feminism – and why it came about. Ask any boy currently how much he knows about the suffragettes, Germaine Greer, Andrea Dworkin and the porn industry or the Sex Discrimination and Equal Pay Acts. I'll guarantee he'll be able to detail the terms and conditions of the Treaty of Versailles or explain what led up to the Second World War, but the sexual politics that have formed the private and public worlds in which he lives probably remain a mystery to him.

In 1998, the Family Planning Association, of which I'm a Patron, held a seminar for parents called Get Sexwise! It confirmed the wealth of academic research, which shows that young people who have good sex education do indeed delay their first sexual activity and are more likely to use protection when they start. And surprisingly, although, perhaps not so surprising given the apparent failures of the school system, a survey of eleven to eighteen year olds showed that most young people – male and female – think the main source of sex education should be their parents. The survey also showed that boys are as nervous and anxious as girls, need as much sympathetic guidance and, given the problems detailed in the Forrest report of getting reliable information from their peers, boys have obviously realised that warm and open parents in the private atmosphere at home are the best people to give that guidance.

So, where do we start? All the evidence indicates that communication between parents and children, which starts early and continues through adolescence, is more effective, more comfortable for both parties and less contentious. It's never a good idea to tell a child they are not old enough to ask questions, as the risk is that they will shut down and turn to their mates (with all the male competitiveness and stereotypes they will inevitably engender), pornography or other sources that may at best be unreliable or inaccurate, at worst distorted and inappropriate. We should though, be guided by our children's questions, so giving them information only when they're interested and in a way that is easy for them to understand.

For instance, a boy who, around the age of three, insisted on opening the door to the milkman wearing only a tee-shirt, and doing a little twirling dance whilst intoning 'Bum, bum, willy, willy' and then collapsing in hysterics was told, calmly and without a hint of anger that the proper word for 'willy' was 'penis' and, whilst people at home might find his little dance amusing, it wasn't the kind of thing that people outside would necessarily like. Indeed, even at home, grandmas might find it a little odd. Thus two important lessons were learned. Nudity is generally reserved for those with whom one is really intimate – other people might not approve – and there are proper terminologies for private parts!

All children are sexual beings. A survey carried out by the Mayo Clinic in 2000 showed that, by the time they are a year old, a third of children will have been observed stimulating their genitals. Boys, typically, pull at their penises. As early as three they begin to wonder about the differences between boys and girls, ask where babies come from, become interested in the shape of their own bodies and, in a home where nakedness is not concealed, that of their parents. It's at this stage that games like doctors and nurses, mummies and daddies, and playing houses become familiar forms of play.

Chrissie told me about her son who, at around the age of four, spent ages upstairs in the room of a friend's daughter. The two mums were just sitting downstairs drinking coffee and chatting when the two children came roaring into the kitchen completely naked and covered in 'spots'. Red felt tip pen was dotted all over each of them and they explained that they had been playing doctors and patients, taking it in turns. Why, asked the mums, had they taken off all their clothes? To do a proper examination, they explained. The mothers handled the situation without expressing any panic or horror, except at how difficult it would be to scrub off the felt tip, recognising that this was an entirely harmless form of inquisitive play.

As long as the children are more or less of the same age and no one seems distressed or upset at what's going on, there is nothing to worry about. If older boys or girls were spending an inordinate amount of time locked away with younger children and the behaviour of the younger child changed, becoming withdrawn or secretive, there would certainly be cause for concern, but innocent sexual exploration among peers is perfectly natural and probably, although none of us can remember that far back, quite pleasurable.

It is worth saying, even to children of this age, that whilst it's good to cuddle, kiss or even stroke, they should always remember that their bodies belong to them and no one else. If they don't like what's happening, they don't have to do it. And if someone makes them feel uncomfortable or if anything scares them, it's OK to come and tell Mum and Dad.

Lauren Roche is a New Zealand doctor who tells the most terrifying story in her book, *Life On the Line*, about her son Christopher who is a serial sex abuser of young children. His abusive behaviour began in his teens – his mother first became aware of it when he abused a relative's eight year old – and has continued into adulthood. At the time of writing, he is serving the latest of a number of prison sentences. Lauren believes that Christopher was drawn into a ring of paedophiles to which he was introduced at a Christian 'Live and Learn' camp when he was only twelve.

When she realised that an older man was taking an inappropriate interest in her son, she managed to stop their contact, and assumed everything would then be all right. But when she discovered her son was inflicting abuse on other children, she found it impossible to get any form of help or treatment for him.

Professor Eileen Vizard, who works with young abusers in this country, says children who abuse other kids have invariably been harmed themselves and she believes that, if the problem is addressed early enough, whilst the abuser is still a child or early teenager, it is possible to offer successful treatment. She is very clear that there is all the difference in the world between children of the same age being inquisitive about each other and the kind of children she deals with. But she emphasises the need to be on the lookout for any distress among young boys who may have been spending a lot of time with much older children, or who have been away on a residential holiday or camp. She also believes it's important to help children to talk openly about their bodies. That way they'll find it much easier to say 'No' to things they don't like and talk to their parents about their worries.

The organisation Planned Parenthood drew up a set of guidelines in 1991 about what kind of things children should know about sex at what age, which may be helpful:

By age five children should:

- Use correct terms for all sexual body parts, including reproductive organs.
- Be able to talk about body parts without a sense of naughtiness.
- Be able to understand and identify concepts of 'maleness' and 'femaleness'.

– Be able to ask trusted adults about sex.
– Know that 'sex-talk' is for private times at home.

At ages six to nine, children should:

– Be aware that all creatures reproduce themselves.
– Have and use acceptable vocabulary for communication about body parts, including their own and that of the opposite sex.
– Be aware that sexual identity includes sexual orientation: lesbian, gay, straight or bisexual.
– Understand the basic facts about AIDS.

(It's worth being aware, if this seems too much for them to cope with, that children mature much earlier physically today than they did in the '50s and '60s – there was a huge scandal in Nicaragua in 2003 when the parents of a nine-year-old pregnant girl who had been raped helped her get a medical abortion. It's also as well for parents to inform their children of some of the dangerous and unpleasant consequences of sex – in a way they can understand – rather than have them pick it up from TV, magazines, the internet or friends.)

At ages nine to thirteen, children should:

– Have an understanding of sexuality as a natural part of life (ages twelve to thirteen).
– View their sexual feelings as legitimate and normal.
– Understand that sex is pleasurable as well as a way to make a baby.
– Realise that sexual acts can be separated from reproductive acts.
– Know about how male and female bodies grow and differ.
– Know about contraception (ways of preventing pregnancy and diseases).
– Know about changes they can expect in their bodies before puberty, such as wet dreams and menstruation (ages nine to eleven).
– Know about sexually transmitted diseases.

An American survey of Adolescent Sexual Behaviour carried out in 1997 seems to suggest that the number of adolescents who say they have had sexual intercourse has levelled off in recent years and may well be declining. The most important factors associated with a delay in 'going all the way' were reported as: a feeling of warmth and caring from parents and family and parental supervision; coming from a two-parent household; having parents who completed their education as far as the equivalent of A level; involvement in athletics for girls; academic success; religion.

It's incredibly hard to know how to begin to approach these questions with your boys even if you are a family that's fairly relaxed about sex and nudity. This attitude changes, by the way, around the age of twelve and it's driven by them not you. As adolescent boys' bodies begin to change, they DO NOT want Mum to see them starkers anymore and they DO NOT want to see you nude either. Accept it. Dig out the dressing gown. There's no point telling them they have a right to privacy when it comes to their own bodies and then expecting them to run around like carefree and unselfconscious five-year-olds for the rest of their lives.

Like me, Charles Jennings, the author of *Father's Race, A Book About Paternity*, has found the car an excellent venue for the discussions that have to take place with his two pre-adolescent sons, but with difficulty.

'I have, once or twice, managed to have one of those pant-wettingly upfront conversations about relationships, feelings for others, sexual intercourse, conception and contraception. The last time it happened, it was in the car. This was a breakthrough, because it meant I could avoid catching anyone's eye in the middle of my speech and embarrassing myself. Being at the wheel also meant that I could use driving as a way of moderating the exchange, introducing delays in which I could check a given train of thought for booby traps.

So the sex talk is pretty straightforward. Broadly, we're all in favour of it, but there are certain protocols and provisos that have to be dealt with. We have the broad moral catch-all that everything is OK as long as it's consensual. Thus I have done my 'Forty Years

On' talk (when you get down there things aren't straightforward at all . . . It's not pretty, but it was put there for a purpose . . . if anyone touches you there that person is wicked), more or less without tensing myself to death. And I have done my pious 'It's the feelings as much as the act itself' rap: about as meaningful as advanced number theory to a pre-adolescent boy.

And I'm aware that there are areas of sexual experience that I know nothing about in a practical sense and so can't advance much advice about. But, illness, illegality and injury aside, I have tried to sound fairly up and optimistic at the same time as I have laboured away at my points. And I am going to be an outstanding source of wisdom on the subject of what happens when girls dump you and why they do and why this is not necessarily the end of the world. The wreckage of teen and early twenties' love affairs/one night stands/disastrous encounters is going to be a topic on which I can dilate more or less endlessly.'

So, given that we now have cheery little chaps who are totally comfortable about saying 'penis' or 'vagina' without choking on their cornflakes, you've said absolutely nothing about the stains on the sheets because wet dreams and masturbation are perfectly normal, they generally seem to have a healthy attitude to women and girls, are beginning to take an interest, and the pictures start to appear on the bedroom wall or you find the magazines under the bed when you go to pick up the stray socks and underpants. What do you do?

For a mother, I think, nothing is harder than acknowledging that her son is now really interested in women and she's not one of them. And then there's that same dilemma that occurs with the sexist jokes – do we knock down their humour as bad and unacceptable, meanwhile portraying ourselves as miserable po-faced old bats with no sense of humour? In this case are we dried up old sticks, who, again, think their interest in sex is wicked and will stop at nothing to slap it down?

Joanna found she had real difficulties with this issue – long before the scantily dressed girls appeared on the walls. She found it, she said,

'Curiously unsettling when he watches Top of the Pops *and I, as a trendy, switched on mum, look at the girls wearing next to nothing and think – that's OK, it's their choice. They look very attractive and empowered – and he looks at me and says, "Yuk, Mum, that's disgusting". I know he's testing me – and to be honest in my heart I'm thinking it's not empowering to be half naked on stage – the guys never are – and I know he's fancying them like crazy and trying to wind me up and I honestly don't know what to say.'*

Linda Bellingham says she gets far more exercised about violence in films and on TV than ever she did about sex. She hasn't had to face the 'smutty' mags question, but did find pictures of

'some bird called Nell something in her smalls on the bedroom walls and I did catch one of them looking at the Internet. I just said, "How sad are you?" and sort of laughed it off. It doesn't seem to have become a problem. The thing I really found upsetting was the rap songs when you hear lyrics which use "bitch" and "cunt" routinely. I totally banned them, explaining that I found them really offensive because there just isn't an equivalent word with which I could put them down that's as graphic or demeaning.'

Jenny Stephen took a typically no-nonsense approach. She told her boys she didn't mind pictures of beautiful women going on the bedroom walls as long as they were clothed. If any nudes appeared, she would stick pictures of penises all over the kitchen walls. She also talked to them about why she might find nudes offensive and why they would be uncomfortable with the penises. 'Always,' she says, 'have the conversation.'

I never had any trouble knowing what to say either. I've interviewed too many young women who were persuaded by their agents that taking their kit off for the camera would do their career no end of good, only to find they were made to feel like a piece of meat and have regretted it. I've never insisted a poster was taken down and only asked that any magazines or pictures should be put away so as not to offend my sensibilities or that of our cleaner, but

I've also, when I've had to confront soft or hard porn in the house, had a discussion about it.

We've talked about the difference between erotica, soft and hard pornography. I've told them about the women I've spoken to who have felt uncomfortable about making porn and about those who have been abused. When they have argued that women choose to do it for money, I've explained to them about coercion and how difficult a lot of women find it to earn a living. It comes as quite a surprise to boys when they realise that 'porn stars' or prostitutes are often women who have been forced into the work by traffickers who promised them a 'better life' or through pimps who control their drug habit or that, in some cases, they are women with children to support who couldn't find any other way to feed them.

I've also talked to them about how uneasy some of the young women I know feel about having these images paraded in front of them (good idea if they're hoping to lure a girl up to their room at any time and don't wish to offend her in any way). Ella Boaden who's a journalist in her early twenties told me:

> *'I have real difficulty with the laddish behaviour I come across at work. You get so mad and embarrassed when they've got Britney Spears half naked on a screensaver, but you don't like to say anything in case they think you've got no sense of humour. This summer I went on holiday with my sister and her boyfriend. I really had to bite my lip when he brought out a set of* Loaded *playing cards decorated with naked women. I knew I was just supposed to see it as "a bit of fun" and if I'd mentioned that I didn't like it, he'd have probably called me a po-faced lesbian.'*

Young women like Ella are not helped by the advertising industry. Last year there were two major campaigns that caused concern. The Pretty Polly interactive ad for matching bras, pants and tights which invited the viewer to touch the model just below the breast and the British International Motor Show ad which implied that men are only interested in two things – cars and women in bras. In both cases, those responsible for the ads were women. Pretty Polly's managing director, Sue Clague, said hers was 'innocent fun'.

Most of the people I talked to felt considerable concern about this ad and the writer and broadcaster Beatrix Campbell found it positively dangerous. 'The bottom line,' she says, 'is that the Pretty Polly advertisement invites men to touch women up and I've got no time for women, now in positions of power, who've bought into that "oafish" lad culture.' They certainly do our poor boys no favours at all. As they try to find their way through what's acceptable and what isn't, this kind of billboard or bus stop soft porn is unfairly confusing for them.

No matter how much you discuss these issues with your boys, they may not give up looking at the pictures, and it is too heavy-handed to ban anything but really offensive hard core porn, but at least they'll know there is an argument to be had on the matter. Their ears really open to that argument when you explain that real girls and women will be impressed by a guy who knows the politics of sexual exploitation, who finds it distasteful to be part of a group of men acting like rutting stags in front of a mucky movie, and who could never be described as a 'creep'. It's sheer bliss, as they get older, when you overhear them chatting with their lovely mature girlfriends, and they trot out all the arguments you've placed at their disposal, basking in the girl-friend's approval.

There is some new research being done, which suggests that looking at porn regularly and over a prolonged period can be harmful. Thaddeus Birchard, a London psychotherapist, says it shouldn't become a problem for those boys who have a family where making good intimate, affectionate relationships has been put in place early on. Masturbating using pornography is, he explains, not bad in itself, as it can bring comfort in a difficult and sometimes painful world, but the evidence suggests that a pre-occupation with pornography occurs where relationships are already difficult and in some boys and young men it can begin to act in the same addictive manner as a drug might.

For boys who are withdrawn and lonely – as indeed is generally the case with older men who become obsessed with pornography – it provides an escape into oblivion. Birchard says when such a boy enters the world of fantasy imagery he doesn't have to face reality.

It provides a protective tunnel in which to escape from the rigours and demands of daily life.

If it does appear to be a problem, if many lonely hours are spent locked away in a room and there's a deeper air of unhappiness than you would expect from the average teenage boy, Birchard advises not adding to what can be a vicious circle. The boy feels bad about himself, so he uses porn to make himself feel better. An angry parent who's disgusted at what she finds will only make him feel worse. Talking and helping him understand what's going on may help. If not, it's a good idea to seek professional help with a counsellor.

One of the biggest anxieties parents have these days about their boys and sex seems to be, 'supposing my boy went too far one night and got accused of rape?' There's been a great deal of controversy about some high profile cases where young men have seemingly been wrongly accused of rape or sexual assault, although the conviction rates for alleged rapists are generally agreed to be far too low. It helps, I believe, for young men to know what the law says and what kind of behaviour is expected of them.

A lot of stuff and nonsense has been written and said about proposals which will change the laws. 'It is now apparently government policy to see more men convicted of rape on less evidence,' wrote one commentator, 'bring on the bedside breathalyser tests.' So, let's just look for a moment at what will be achieved by the proposed changes to the Sexual Offences Act, which might be expected to become law in the near future. Firstly, the word 'consent' will effectively be removed from the law and it will have to be shown, where a rape has been alleged, that a woman did not give her 'free agreement' to penetrative sex. This does not, as many people have wrongly claimed, mean that the burden of proof will shift from the accuser to the accused.

As Jennifer Temkin, Professor of Law at Sussex University and the author of *Rape and the Legal Process*, points out, the prosecution will still have to prove beyond reasonable doubt that the woman did not agree which means that the defendant will only be expected to have taken reasonable steps to ensure that the sex was not coercive. The law works perfectly well in Canada and New Zealand and, as Temkin, asks, is it unreasonable, if you are intimate enough to have sex with someone, just to have a conversation about whether you're both OK about it?

What this small change to the language and the intent of the law means is the modernisation of the nineteenth-century concept embodied in the word 'consent'. It was surely time we got rid of the idea – and boys really need to understand that times have changed – that men push for it and women take it.

What is intended in the reforms is that we have a legal definition which assumes sex is about two people freely agreeing to enjoy each where both are in a position to initiate proceedings, but to respect a 'No' if one doesn't feel like it. Rape is now to be more clearly defined as a violent and reckless act where free agreement is absent.

The intent of the new rules is also to dispense with the old defence of 'honest belief' that a woman consented to sex. If you're talking iniquity, this 'defence' really takes the biscuit. Short skirt? She was asking for it. Not a virgin? Must be a slut. Met him in a pub? What nice girl would be out drinking? No serious injury? Well, she can't have suffered any great trauma. I once sat in court and heard a woman describe meeting a man in a pub, having a few drinks, going home for coffee, making it quite plain she didn't want to sleep with him and asking him to leave. She went on to explain how she had cried out, pushed him away and said 'No' time and time again. And he agreed she had done all those things, but he thought women always had to put up a fight, even when they really wanted it. So he 'honestly believed' that she had consented at the time, although he now realised he had made a mistake. Acquitted!

And so to the breathalyser by the bed and an end to the sixteen vodkas school of seduction. The idea that a woman who is dead drunk, asleep or unconscious is not in a state to agree to sex seems to me blindingly obvious and as a legal concept was recognised even by Victorian judges. Falling into bed tipsy with willing participation is one thing, given that you both agree that sex is on the agenda, but slipping a Mickey Finn or Rohypnol – the date rape drug – into someone's drink with the intention of rendering her incapable of resistance, is quite another thing.

It is most important that we get this message across to our boys.

That accepting a drink isn't asking for it. That a shag is not an automatic consequence of a night out if he's paid for drinks or dinner: that's prostitution. That 'No' means 'No' and an 'honest belief' that she was really saying 'Maybe' now means 'it's straight to jail without passing Go'.

One young man, the writer Sean Thomas, got a lot of publicity when the law reform was first mooted by arguing that there is a mismatch in the expectations of men and women when it comes to sexual encounters. He believes women are naïve about what men want in the bedroom and, he says, they need to treat male sexuality with more respect and understanding. In a discussion on *Woman's Hour* he said, 'They need to realise that if you lie naked next to a man in bed, then chances are he's going to get aroused and demand sex.' This seems to me another example of men doing themselves a disservice by displaying themselves as unreconstructed primates whose hormones will always overrule their grey matter.

David Aaronovitch, formerly of *The Independent*, now of *The Guardian*, is obviously a little more advanced on the evolutionary ladder. He once wrote in his column of an encounter he'd had as a student. It was with a woman he described as 'gorgeous'. They spent many nights in bed. They kissed and cuddled and she made it clear, he said, without saying it out loud, that she wanted nothing more. 'When in doubt,' he added, 'leave it out. If you're wrong she can always put you straight.' At last, I thought when I read his words, a man who is prepared to be the guardian of his own sexual urges and go public with his wisdom. Would there were more like him.

It also seems to me to be important to talk to our older boys about what options remain should they be involved in a sexual relationship where the method of contraception fails or has been forgotten in the heat of the moment and a pregnancy results. They will have no rights whatsoever in influencing the woman's choice – and quite rightly. It is, after all, her body that has to undergo any termination or birth and it has generally in the past been the girl who has been left holding the baby.

The law allows for termination up to twenty-four weeks with the agreement of two doctors. Emergency contraception is available within seventy-two hours of a possible conception and does not count as an abortion, as any fertilised embryo will not yet have implanted. Termination up to twelve weeks can be carried out at a day patient clinic using vacuum aspiration, which sucks out any foetal material. A later abortion involves an induced delivery of an identifiable foetus. Women seem to vary in their emotional attitudes to abortion. Some feel no guilt and only relief; others report feelings of sadness and loss many years later. There are rarely health complications in this country as long as the abortion has been carried out professionally and after care advice has been followed.

Good, responsible boys would want to be involved in helping their partner come to a decision about whether it were possible or not for them both to be involved in becoming parents. Boys need to know before they embark on a sexual relationship that part of being old enough to become physically and emotionally involved with another human being means being responsible enough to face the consequences of what might happen and it's my view that, given the problems with sex education at school (encountered earlier in this chapter), parents are best placed to make sure they have this kind of hard-headed advice.

The Child Support Agency, established in the early '90s, laid down a legal framework whereby fathers, even absent ones, are considered financially responsible for any offspring. I've always impressed upon my lads that any pleasurable, but reckless encounter can lead to a lifetime of emotional and financial responsibility for a dependant human being. Prevention or abstention is generally better than the cure.

It's often hardest for parents to talk to their children about the pleasurable side of sex, although an old friend of mine and a man who has the easiest, most relaxed relationships with women I've ever witnessed, remembers his father sitting him down and telling him that making love to a woman was the most beautiful thing he had ever known – words the son never forgot. Some mothers have the kind of close and easy relationship with their boys that led one friend's son to ask her if she'd supply his condoms for his first holiday alone at 17; another friend's student son asked his mother to buy his condoms on special offer at Tesco's because they were too expensive to buy on student funds (the free ones on the NHS, apparently, are not nearly good enough quality!). Most of us don't begin to approach such easy intimacy.

Sunday Surgery, the Radio One programme I mentioned in Chapter Three, is noticing a significant rise in the number of boys and young men phoning or e-mailing to ask just the kind of intimate question that it's tough to put to their parents. Callers often express the kind of awkwardness that leaps from the page of John Hegley's poem:

> *There's a girl at school*
> *I love up to the sky,*
> *I want to say she's elegant*
> *And other words she cannot spell,*
> *But I just tell her she stinks.*

The show's producer, Sam Steele, tells me,

> *'When I started on the show eighteen months ago it would be very rare for a boy to talk on air about anything to do with his physical health, specifically to mention the word "penis". Now our e-mail box is full of messages from boys absolutely terrified about the changes going on in their bodies, specifically their penis during puberty, and needing to know whether their emissions are normal or not. What size is the right size etc?'*

In addition to the advice given on the show there is also a free and confidential helpline, staffed by a team of trained counsellors. The number is 0800 110 100 and they are happy to talk to parents as well as kids.

The Internet is also a mine of information for boys and young men looking for information about topics not generally discussed with parents or in sex education classes, such as falling in love, breaking up, orgasms, wet dreams and how to give a partner sexual pleasure. The authors of 'The Effects of Internet Sexuality on Children and Adolescents', a section in the new book *Sex and the Internet*, edited by Al Cooper, are reassuring about those young people who can 'filter out accurate from distorted information for whom the Internet can be an incredibly rich source of information'.

But they warn that 'for those teenagers unable to tell fact from fiction, the Internet, with its vast amount of distorted sexual stimuli, pornography and information, may only serve to propagate more misinformation and reinforce exaggerated beliefs about sexuality.' The authors recommend looking out for well run sites where young people might be able to chat to each other. 'America Online and other websites have teen monitors for teen chats. This monitoring gives teenagers a chance to be experts and take positions of responsibility.'

It can be especially difficult for young homosexuals who are often forced by the atmosphere at school – where they can be regarded as deviant – and sometimes by fears of parental opposition, to live in a kind of twilight world. For them, too, the net can provide vital information, but it is also fraught with danger.

James is an extremely liberal and open-minded parent, but he became worried when his fourteen-year-old son ran up an enormous mobile phone bill. He checked the itemised details and found he had been calling gay chat lines. His son found it hard to be open even with a father who, although cross about the size of the bill, was not censorious about the possibility that his son might be gay. It emerged eventually that the boy had also been connecting with chat rooms on the Internet and had arranged to meet men he'd communicated with there. When he had said, on one occasion, that he was staying at a friend's house – and his father had seen no reason to doubt him – he had in fact been staying with an older man in an hotel. The boy was not visibly harmed by the experience except to say that it felt very underhand and made him feel used and dirty. His father was heartbroken that it was the only way his son had felt able to explore his sexuality.

James was also at a loss as to how to help his boy, although he knew instinctively that he needed to meet other young people going through similar experiences with whom he could explore his feelings. There are two respected organisations in this country, which advise parents and friends of young gays and lesbians on how best to help them find a life of their own in safety. FFLAG – Family and Friends of Young Lesbians and Gays operate a busy helpline: 01454 852418, an e-mail service info@fflag.org.uk and a website www.fflag.org.uk. Parents/Friends can be reached on 01902 820497 and their website is www.parentsfriend.demon.co.uk

It would be a pity if children were denied access to the useful parts of the Internet, such as monitored chat rooms dedicated to their own age group, because of parental fears about what they might encounter whilst on line. So it's wise to be clued up about what dangers lurk there and how to avoid them. A US survey of children aged ten to seventeen revealed that many experienced distressing encounters online, rangeing from unwanted e-mails and harassment to aggressive sexual solicitations. The researchers found that, during a one-year period, one in five experienced unwanted sexual solicitation or approach over the Internet; one in thirty received aggressive sexual solicitations; one in four experienced unwanted exposure to pictures of nudes or people having sex; one in seventeen was threatened or harassed.

It's not difficult for children and teens to come upon pornographic websites and sexually explicit material. This can happen in a number of ways, for instance, mistaken or mistyped URLS: a simple mistake such as typing 'playstatiom.com' instead of 'playstation.com' can take a child to an adult site. Simple search words, such as 'whitehouse', 'toys', 'pets', 'boys' or 'girls', can lead them astray. Innocent use of search engines can lead to adult-oriented sites, and 'push' pornography and e-mails can land in their inboxes. If they open the e-mails they can end up at pornographic sites.

There are signs of problematic Internet use among the young that parents should watch out for: excessive use that leads to neglect of personal relationships and isolation; acute or chronic depression; the search for repeated mood-altering experiences leading to a high; a history of sexual behaviour problems and a lack of or little engagement in social activities with friends.

Cooper's *Sex and the Internet*, offers a useful Guide to Safety and Prevention for Parents:

– *Talk with your child, long before adolescence, about sexuality. Part of the reason sexual content on the Internet is so compelling for children and teenagers is because so few adults are willing to talk to them.*

- *Don't put computers with Internet access in a child's room. Instead, keep the computer with Internet access in a public place where there is lots of activity at home and where the use can be easily monitored such as a family room or kitchen.*
- *Use software that provides the best security and precaution against accessing adult-oriented sites, including ones that will track the child's use of the internet and sites visited. Look for newer or updated versions periodically. Test software that claims to block children's access to adult-oriented materials on the Internet. When it comes to software and blocking devices be a good consumer. What are the comparative ratings? Which programmes are the most popular? See if you can beat the software and blocking programmes. If you can, you can guarantee your child will be able to as well. Ask other parents what they use. There are several software packages such as Cyberpatrol, Internet Watchdog, SurfWatch, SafeSurf, CYBERsitter and Net Nanny that serve as blocking software, filtering software and tracking software.*
- *Provide children and teens with age-appropriate alternatives. Help children explore what is out there in cyberspace. Visit a variety of sites with the child while he or she is online. You are bound to come across undesirable sites and that can be a good 'teaching moment' as you discuss what is good and bad about the site.*
- *Teach children and teens to keep their identity private and never to give out personal information on the Internet. Medaris (2000) demonstrates that within forty-five minutes of identifying a child with an e-mail address only, a sexual predator can discover the child's home address, phone number, where the child goes to school and other particulars.*
- *Get to know your child's online friends. Advise youth NEVER to meet people in person they have met online.*
- *Advise them there is never complete privacy on the Internet.*
- *Make sure the child's computer time is limited. People, not computers should be their best friends.*

- *Set and discuss online rules with children about computer times, usage and so on. When a child violates the rules and conditions, remove the child's privilege of Internet access, including, if necessary, prohibiting [the child] from going to friends' homes and libraries that have Internet access and tell the school about the temporary ban.*
- *Learn enough about computers to enjoy them with your child.*
- *Make sure children feel comfortable enough with you to come and ask questions. Ask them to show you where they go online.*
- *Keep children out of chat rooms or monitor their involvement in youth-oriented chat rooms.*
- *Teach children and teens about the incidence of credit card fraud on the Internet.*
- *Teach children never to respond to e-mail, chat comments, or newsgroup messages that are hostile, belligerent and inappropriate or in any way make them feel uncomfortable.*
- *If your child is being pursued or harassed by someone online or is engaging in sexual activities with a person online, report it to the police.*

There's one simple question about sex I've left till last, probably because it was the most frequently asked by all the parents I spoke to. When do I agree to let a girlfriend stay overnight? India Knight was the most openly welcoming of the whole idea of her sons' sexuality.

'Can't say I'm madly looking forward to any of this. Sex . . . mmmm . . . I'll be glad I suppose – the last thing you want is to have some red-faced, bumbling son who has difficulties with girls and who walks around pent up with longing all day. I'd like them to have lots of girlfriends and become relatively experienced (rather a creepy thing to say, but I do feel so desperately sorry for boys who didn't have enough sex as adolescents – it leaves a sort of mark you can see in adulthood). But I wouldn't want any information whatsoever. Sleepover girlfriends: yes, reluctantly, because I was so often a sleepover girlfriend myself!'

I'm afraid I never quite shared India's relatively easy acceptance, but I did develop a strategy which I hoped would ensure our survival through our children's teens, based on parental collusion. All you have to do is ensure that all the parents of a circle of friends have each other's phone numbers to hand all the time, and that you talk to each other. So, when a group of spotty oiks sat around my kitchen table discussing when it would be OK to spend the night with their girlfriend in their parents' home, I came up with the following answer to this knotty question:

It's not fair to ask me to take responsibility for the welfare of another child. I'm not prepared to take at face value assurances that, 'It's OK, Mum and Dad know exactly where I am.' I'll only allow it (assuming first that both boy and girl are over the age of sixteen, as before that it's illegal), after I've personally spoken to the girl's parents and they've agreed. Thus I'm off the hook until hell freezes over or they're all past the age of majority. At eighteen I reckon what they do is pretty much their own business and you can only hope you've brought 'em up right. I have to say I was impressed and pleased that the boys were thinking about it and felt they could trust me enough to be asking.

CHAPTER FIVE

BULLY BOYS

'At the Suzy Lamplugh Trust we so often get calls from parents, teachers and employers wanting to talk about personal safety for girls and women and they are often very surprised when we say "what about the boys/male members of staff?" There is almost an assumption that they will somehow cope and that perhaps it is all part of "growing up" for boys to "fight their battle" along the way.'

Ann Elledge is the trust manager at the organisation set up by Diana Lamplugh after her daughter, Suzy, a young London estate agent, was abducted and almost certainly murdered by a man she had agreed to show around a house. Its aim is to research and advise on aggression and violence and help people protect themselves. They are only too aware that the group most at risk is young males aged sixteen to twenty-four, partly because this is when young men begin to get involved with alcohol and start to go out in large groups, but mainly because boys are especially in danger, as, unlike girls, they tend not to be taught how to look after themselves.

As Ann says,

'*Unfortunately there is still a feeling that it isn't macho to take evasive action when an aggressive situation is developing. Most young women have been warned of the dangers they may face and will tend to think in advance about protecting themselves. Most of the girls, if they see a group standing on a street corner that they feel themselves threatened by, will cross over to the other side, whilst most young men feel they have to walk straight through the middle of them. When we talk to groups, both at mixed and all boys' schools, they have terrible tales to tell, but many of them feel they shouldn't own up to having felt threatened or scared by a situation.'*

One of the parents I spoke to, Tariq Ali, tells an amusing story about an evening when his older daughter went out with a group of friends and they saw a gang of youths hanging about on the street.

'They knew boys without girls ran a greater risk of violence. Boys and young men are more likely to be the victims of violence than anyone else in society and the girls just seemed to know this instinctively. So the girls all phoned to say they'd be home a bit late, because they had to walk the boys home!'

The tales the boys have to tell can indeed be terrible. The research shows that boys are at risk primarily from fights, which can break out on the street, and from muggings, when increasingly weapons are being used. Work published in 2000 by the University of London shows that in a sample of 2,500 young males, 51 per cent said they had experienced physical abuse outside the home in the form of being kicked, slapped or hit with an implement.

We've all heard the stories about what now seems routine in the inner cities. Ann told me about one of the Trust's trainers whose fourteen-year-old son has been mugged four times in the past year in central London. Another, who lives in Hackney, got into the habit of driving her son to the tube station, carrying his bike on the car. They would lock up the bike on the railings outside the Underground because she would be at work later in the afternoon when he came back from school and he would need to cycle home. They would say goodbye at the entrance to the station.

Every day he was 'roughed up' on the stairs going down to the platform. His travel card was taken from him and he was constantly asked for his mobile phone or for money. Eventually she started taking him down to the train and seeing him safely on board and she noticed another parent was doing exactly the same with his son. They have now reported the incidents to London Transport who are looking at CCTV and hope to catch the perpetrators, but as Ann says, these are just a couple of examples of how grim London, Manchester, Birmingham or Bristol can now be for young males.

In inner London and Manchester, the two areas I know best, it's now common practice for a boy to wear the cheapest and naffest watch he can find and carry two mobiles and two wallets. The active mobile and wallet with money in it are kept secreted about the boy's person. An old mobile with no SIM card and an empty wallet, kept where they are easily accessible, would be given up in the event of a mugging. My own boys have always gone out with enough money for a taxi home tucked into their socks in case of disaster. It's dreadful and frightening that they have to take such evasive action, but it's far more sensible to have something to give up and to hand it over willingly than to try and 'take on' the muggers. That can only lead to greater danger.

There is no point in trying to do what every parent is tempted to do – keep them home or drive them everywhere and always pick them up. They need to learn how to negotiate the world in which they are going to live as adults. But it is up to us as parents to make sure they are equipped with the kind of knowledge and strategies that will keep them as safe as it's possible to be.

Ann and Diana believe that we have to start teaching our boys about self-preservation from a young age. They both worry a lot about the misconceptions the Stranger Danger message gives out. There are, they say, some horrendous websites, which give out completely the wrong idea about what a stranger looks like. As a result of the popular propaganda, if you ask a child to draw a stranger, he or she will invariably portray a man with a beard who looks threatening. If you show children a picture of a woman with a briefcase, they will say she couldn't possibly present any danger because she is a woman. Quite how this message has gained currency after Myra Hindley and the Moors' murders escapes me completely, yet children are still being made to fear strange men but are not warned about the risks posed by some women or, indeed, by people within their family, circle of friends or neighbourhood – people who might be expected to be completely trustworthy.

The Trust advocates starting with boys as young as two – from when they can walk independently – and teaching them to think about risk assessment. None of us would dream of failing to drum into them the Green Cross Code, or to teach them about negotiating traffic when we're out and about. It's automatic to point out, say, that we don't cross the road here because there are too many parked cars around which we can't see, and instead we head for a proper crossing or an area where looking right, left and right again gives a clearer view. Teaching about reducing other forms of risk can take place in a similar vein.

It can begin, for example, if you are in a shop or precinct where you can discuss with your boy what he might do if he loses Mummy or Daddy in the supermarket. We all witnessed, in the horrific video of Jamie Bulger being led to his death by two other young boys, how trusting small children of this age can be. His was also a tragic example of threat coming from an unexpected source. Without frightening them, we can, when we are going about everyday business, chat, seemingly casually, about possible scenarios and the best way to handle them. 'Just supposing we were in the town and we lost each other . . . Just supposing we were at the seaside and because the beach was really busy, we couldn't find each other. Where would you head for?'

I have personal experience of how easily a young child can be there one minute and gone the next. When Charlie was two and Edward six we were on holiday in the South of France. I had eaten a raw seafood platter the night before with the inevitable consequence – death would have been a welcome release. David agreed to let me stay in bed whilst I slowly recovered and he took the children to the beach, arranging to come back at lunchtime. By then I was feeling a little better and was up and dressed when the door to the flat we were staying in burst open and a panicked Dave and Ed gasped out that they had lost Charlie.

At first I thought they were joking and expected a grinning little face to appear round the door, exclaiming, 'Fooled you!', but it quickly became obvious they were serious. They had been walking up through the pedestrian precinct between the beach and the flat when they stopped for a moment to readjust the burden of beach bags, lilos, balls and all the other paraphernalia you need for a morning's entertainment at the seaside. In the few seconds that they turned around, the spot where Charlie had been standing became empty. They had looked around everywhere but couldn't find him. A nearby shopkeeper and his wife had tried to be helpful, realising their panic, but neither David nor Ed had the French to communicate with them. I did. We rushed out to the shop.

The couple called the police and the local radio station, reassuring me that this kind of thing happened all the time and we shouldn't worry. Locals knew that the local radio station was the central communication point for missing children and they were sure he would turn up unharmed. They advised that I should stay on the spot, in case Charlie remembered where he had last been and came back, whilst David and the shopkeeper went on a search. I have never spent such an agonising two hours, imagining my baby abducted, hurt and possibly killed. I walked up and down the street, crying his name like a demented banshee.

There was, of course, for us a happy ending. A call from the local radio station told us they had a small blonde boy who seemed not to understand anything that was said to him. We piled into the shopkeeper's van and he drove us to the other side of town where Charlie stood, utterly bemused, in the station reception area. We don't know to this day what happened to him; the young couple who had brought him to the station were just driving off in their car when I rushed out to ask them where and how they had found him. They gave a breezy wave and shouted it was no trouble. Charlie was speechless and still can't remember where he was for two hours, although he was physically unharmed.

We were lucky, but it's an object lesson in how better preparation, even in one so young, might have avoided the worst of the problems. The Suzy Lamplugh Trust recommend discussing with children who they would go to if something similar were to happen to them. If it happens in a supermarket, the child should go to the checkout, tell the person on the till and wait there with them until the parents are told of the child's whereabouts. In a shopping precinct they should look for a security guard in uniform or walk into the nearest shop and talk to the owner or shop assistant (which is what Charlie should have been told).

On a beach they should find a lifeguard, police officer or shop-keeper. It's most important that they know never to ask anyone for assistance who is not in an identifiable position of authority or who is not obviously employed by the establishment in which they are lost. They should never go off with someone they don't know, male, female or child, no matter how sweet the inducements offered, and should never accept invitations, even from people they know and trust, without talking to their parents first. If something does happen that frightens them or makes them feel uncomfortable, or if someone appears to be forcing them to do something they don't want, they should get home as quickly as they can if it's possible; if not, they should shout and scream for help.

The Suzy Lamplugh Trust has made a video for teenagers to give them some idea of how they might negotiate difficulties when they begin to go out clubbing. The boys who've seen the video – street-wise kids of fifteen and sixteen – have, in the course of discussions about the film, described it as revelatory, generally agreeing that they wished they'd had such discussion and advice much earlier, at around the age of thirteen. (The video, by the way, can be sent free to schools.)

The video shows various scenes, which demonstrate how aggressive people can become when they are drinking, especially when they are high on the atmosphere of heavy music and possibly showing off in front of girls. It asks the viewers to think about how they are going to get home, especially if not fully in control after drinking. The film demonstrates how to avoid confrontational situations and recommends always letting your parents know where you are going.

In the early part of the discussions, the boys were apparently quite blasé and arrogant, especially dismissive of the suggestion that they should let their mums know where they are going. As the discussion progressed they began to open up and voice their concerns. They often revealed that they had been mugged or even beaten up and talked about how threatening and frightening such experiences had been. They also began to recognise that their behaviour – being confident, but not arrogant and avoiding, rather than inviting, confrontation – could have made all the difference.

The boys even conceded, reluctantly, that their mums have their best interests at heart and need to know where their sons are in case something goes wrong. They also realised that booking a (licensed) taxi in advance and keeping enough money to pay for it in a safe place (socks again) makes sense. It can be expensive, but I have never let my boys go out without emergency money and they know better than to spend it on anything other than getting home safely. I also always tell them that a mobile phone, a wallet or a watch are not worth risking your life over. Possessions are replaceable. They are not.

Ann Elledge recommends keeping communication about these issues going as the boys grow up and raising them in the course of normal conversation just to remind them of their possible vulnerability. That way you can avoid the idea that it's just 'Mum nagging on again'. She doesn't encourage sending boys to self-defence or martial arts classes, as they may engender the wrong attitude. It is always, she says, dangerous to meet aggression with aggression, but she doesn't rule out such classes if they seem to be improving a boy's confidence. If you look confident, you are less likely to become a victim. If you do go down this route, check out the classes carefully. The emphasis in any good karate or judo class should be on self-defence, not attack. The atmosphere should be non-aggressive and well-controlled and the teacher should constantly remind the boys that avoiding the need for self-defence is always their priority.

Ann also encourages boys to practise not 'giving the eye', which can be an open invitation to some young men to have a go. A boy walking in the street should appear confident and in control and should learn how to make eye contact, without inviting comment or aggressive behaviour by holding the look too long. It's not necessary to avoid eye contact altogether and walk with eyes down, as this can give the impression of fear and weakness.

If the worst does happen and a boy is attacked, the Trust recommends being observant and 'clocking your muggers'. The next step, always, as soon as possible after the incident is to tell the parents, sharing as much detailed description with them as possible; then the parents should make a report to the police and the schools in the area. The effects of a mugging may not show immediately, but can be very upsetting some days later when a boy might shake and grow agitated and nervy. Doing something about it is a positive counter to feeling powerless and, as Ann says, getting the police and schools involved is the only way in the long run that we will put a stop to this kind of crime.

It is, of course, extremely difficult to help boys become confident, non-violent human beings if they live in an atmosphere where violence is endemic in the home or where boys who aren't prepared to put their fists up and 'fight like men' are considered cissies. We still have a long way to go in changing boys' thinking on who constitutes a hero – all their role models are action men who fight their way out of trouble – Bruce Willis, Arnold Schwarzenegger, Rambo, to name but three – and their attitudes to domestic violence can be quite alarming. We saw in the Zero Tolerance Research (see page 87) how common it is for boys to condone sexual violence against women. Similar results are apparent in a number of studies on domestic violence.

A significant percentage believe it's OK to hit a woman if she is disrespectful or unfaithful and this kind of thinking has not been discouraged by a legal system which is lenient towards men who have killed their wives and claim to have been provoked, but does not display a similarly sympathetic attitude towards women who have killed their husbands, even if they acted after suffering years of abuse. There have been a number of high profile cases in recent years where a man has murdered a woman in a frenzied attack, has been found guilty of the lesser charge of manslaughter and received a light prison sentence because he argued that her nagging or her infidelity caused him temporarily to lose his cool. Women who kill are generally believed to have acted in a pre-meditated fashion rather than in the heat of the moment and have to attempt to defend themselves on grounds of diminished responsibility.

The law is now under review and the Solicitor General, Harriet Harman, believes the provocation defence is a 'relic of a previous age'. Ninety five per cent of domestic homicides are carried out by men and Ms Harman was quoted in one newspaper article as saying, 'men kill their wives, generally speaking, out of anger and women kill their husbands out of fear'. She is proposing a new defence of 'self-defence' for women who kill violent husbands and the Director of Public Prosecutions is to urge prosecutors to charge all wife killers with murder instead of manslaughter. Ms Harman believes the provocation defence unfairly blames victims. She has said, 'Men say: "The woman wound me up, she was planning to leave me and I was upset and therefore I am not guilty of murder." Even if a woman has done all those things, it doesn't justify violence – let alone violence to the point of death.'

In the Gender Studies I discussed in Chapter Four, boys would be made aware of these legal and political issues that so affect their lives and those of the people around them. There are already some schemes in schools to raise awareness of domestic violence and there are plenty of opportunities for discussing the issues in other lessons. The statistics could come into maths, and literature is peppered with incidents of domestic violence, which would make useful starting points for discussion. Why does Henleigh Grandcourt turn into such a controlling monster from the moment he has a wedding ring on Gwendolen Harleth's finger in George Elliott's *Daniel Deronda*? Is Othello justified in strangling Desdemona because he suspects she's been unfaithful? And does Soames have the right to rape his wife in *The Forsyte Saga*? Any provision in schools, though, is patchy at the moment. Until it improves, it's for us as parents to make our children aware that the world is changing and domestic violence is simply not acceptable any more.

Boys will invariably argue that men suffer domestic violence, too, and to a small degree, they are right. But they do need to learn that domestic violence has historically been about power and control and existed during many thousands of years during which women were seen as their father's, brother's, or husband's property, to be used and abused at will. I have looked very carefully into research on gender and domestic violence and found that the only study, carried out by MORI in the '80s, which is often quoted as showing that more men than women suffer domestic violence, did not examine the quality of the violence.

Men reported being slapped (we have to remember it has often been considered quite sexy for a woman to slap a man across the face – it's been a feature of many a Hollywood movie as the prelude to passionate reconciliation – prompting the old cliché, 'My God, you're beautiful when you're angry'); and having things thrown at them. These incidents counted as domestic violence. There were no reports of broken limbs, black eyes and hospitalisation. It is generally the case that when a woman is violently angry, she expresses her anger at a distance – hence the plate throwing – but rarely makes a close physical attack on a male who is generally bigger and stronger. Women, on the other hand, do frequently end up in hospital and two a week die as a result of domestic violence.

Anna Jakubiak is the mother of five boys – Christopher who's twenty-three, Antoni aged eighteen, Sam who's fourteen, Daniel aged eight, Alex, a six-year-old, and her last child, Isabella, a four-year-old girl. Anna now works with the Westminster Domestic Violence Forum on bringing the issue into schools. She agreed to tell me about her experiences of living with two extremely violent men, and to explain how she managed to help her boys deal with the domestic violence they witnessed and avoid following the same pattern themselves.

The father of her first three boys had been her childhood sweetheart, but he got involved with drugs in the late '80s when Sam was tiny. Anna believes it was crack, which was given to him by a friend. Within weeks he was hooked and immediately became violent. He suffered, she says, from a drug-induced psychosis. Because she knew he was ill and he had never been violent before and because she loved him and wanted to help, she stayed around much longer than she should.

It was his effect on the boys that finally made her escape for good. From the age of nine, Christopher had seen his mother knocked unconscious and was also on the receiving end of his father's anger and his need to control. Christopher would be told, 'Look what you and your mother have made me do', and still, as a young adult, he says to his mother how much he wishes as a child he had tried to say or do something that might have stopped his father. Anna reassures him this was not possible for such a small boy and would only, probably, have led to even worse violence, possibly even putting himself at risk.

On the day she escaped, the two younger boys had spent the day huddled together in a corner. Their father had shouted at them all day and been verbally abusive for some time. Anna knew it was only a matter of time before he became physically abusive to them. She escaped to a refuge and eventually established herself on her own. The children have not seen their father since Sam, the youngest, was two.

The family lived alone for five years during which Anna spent a lot of time with the boys trying to repair the damage. She concentrated most of her efforts on Christopher, believing that if she focussed on the eldest child, who had been more aware of the abuse, and handled things well with him, the effects would trickle down to the youngest. She has always talked to them all a great deal and explained why she thinks things went so wrong in as honest a way as she could. During the tough times living in various refuges Christopher did break down at one time and talked to a teacher about what had been happening. Anna welcomed the opportunity to share her troubles with a sympathetic and helpful outsider. The teacher managed, with a lot of affection and encouragement, to alleviate Christopher's sense of guilt about not being able to protect his mother, and to make him feel safe again.

Eventually, though, Anna began to worry that the boys needed a masculine influence in their lives, but hers is a cautionary tale when it comes to selecting the wrong or the right kind of male role model. When she met a friend of her brother's who was her age and seemed personable she began a serious relationship with him and had Daniel, her fourth son. For a while they seemed to be developing a normal family life.

Looking back on it now, Anna believes the older boys could sense the tension early on in the relationship, but she did not see it coming. She has no truck with the idea that women who are victims of domestic violence seek out relationships with other violent men, but she does believe that if you have suffered domestic violence once you can easily become a target again. Abusers, she says, can spot a victim with ease and she believes that, after her first experience, her self-esteem and judgement were so shaken and she was so desperate to make everything happy for her children and forget what had happened in the past, she was easy prey for another dangerous man who wanted to control her.

This time, though, after the first episode of violence, she went straight to a solicitor, got an injunction and after a bitter court battle agreed that Daniel should have supervised visits to his father. The other children don't see him at all. The two youngest children, Alex and Isabella, are the result of Anna's current relationship with Michael who she says is a good and gentle man who has provided an excellent 'significant male' for her boys, but they don't live together.

Anna's struggle to bring up decent and gentle young men against impossible odds is inspiring and instructive:

'I suppose I've been tougher on Christopher than on any of the others, working on this principle that if I could get it right with him, it would influence the others. Conversely, if he went off the rails, what chance would I have with the others? He didn't get away with much, but my clear boundaries were his security. I was always strict about bed times, routines, what was acceptable and what was not. I've told them that if they appear too full of themselves or are mouthy or cheeky they will invite trouble and it's always better to avoid it.

I've always insisted that they take a full part in what has to be done around the house. It was quite funny really because one friend of Antoni's practically fainted when they had to do the washing up. But it is in my view the best way to teach them to respect women, to realise that mothers are not there to be their servants, but to guide and protect them until they are old enough to do it for themselves.

I've had to become very tough and independent and I think they admire me for that. I had to learn to do all the things a man would do around the house and they always say how proud they are that I can put up shelves and cupboards and do the decorating. It's important that they see me coping. They've often said that their friends comment on how amazing it is that I cope the way that I do and that I'm always there for them.'

Anna's also convinced that her attitude to violence has been helpful to the boys in enabling them to handle themselves without recourse to their fists.

'There is an absolute no fighting rule. They know that if an older one ever hits a little one, it's bullying and gets no sympathy from me. If a squabble develops into a battle, everyone involved is punished – that way you make sure no-one is winding up somebody else to deliberately get them into trouble. I take away the Playstation or ban TV for a week. It has been difficult to sustain if there's been a man around – they seem to think knowing how to fight is the "making of a man" and they encourage the rough and tumble, and they worry that a boy who can't fight won't be able to stand up for himself. But they're wrong. Chris especially is a shy and sensitive type and not naturally aggressive at all.

I think my example helped Chris when, like so many other boys, he was mugged. He was fifteen and it was a gang of kids who were younger and smaller than him. He's very big, a gentle giant really, and they made him take his shoes off and threatened him with a knife and a knuckle duster. It was all about intimidation and control. I've always told Chris that if anything like that happens he shouldn't fight, but try to talk his way out of it calmly. He did all the right things and told me about it when he came home.

At first he was upset and then he got angry. He decided that we would report it to the school – the boys were from there – so he knew them and he decided he wanted to press charges. I wouldn't have pushed him to do that, it's not considered very street cred to tell the authorities, but he made his own mind up and I supported him. He handled himself very well in court and two of the boys were found guilty. It was very good for Chris. He ended up neither a victim nor an aggressor. I like to think he had the confidence to do what he did because he had seen me use the law to protect myself when I took out an injunction against my partner. He also, because of his experiences at home, recognised that violence can have a terrible effect on people and that the only way to stop it is to tell about it and make sure people who do it are brought to book.'

Anna's policy of Zero Tolerance makes complete sense to me as it does to Martin Stephen both at home and at the school he runs. Any boy caught fighting there is immediately suspended. A second offence means expulsion and there are no excuses. To those who argue that play fighting and rough and tumble come naturally to boys and are an important part of their development, he has a devastating response.

> 'I really don't know what people mean by "play fighting". You never hear people talking about "play rape" do you? So why are we happy to endorse any form of violence as an acceptable way to amuse yourself? Even if it's true that there is joshing and physical contact between boys which starts out as a game, it is simply too dangerous to approve it. A game can quickly become serious and that's when people get hurt. It is never acceptable.
>
> Zero Tolerance is as much a statement of intent as it is a practical policy. I have no doubt boys do engage in some covert fighting, but the policy lets the boys know exactly what is expected of them and exactly what is unacceptable. If you land a blow, in any context, we will take action. What we've found is the boys respond to the simplicity of those rules and ideas. If there are boys who are very physical and have a naturally aggressive tendency – and they do exist – usually they're the "alpha males" – stick them on the rugby or the football field where they can let off steam and show off their physical prowess in a carefully controlled environment where there is a clear set of rules.'

Linda Bellingham also had to endure physical and mental bullying at the hands of her husband. Their separation and the reasons for it became very public because of her fame and the irony of the fact that she had been portraying the 'happy families' Oxo Mum whilst living through the very opposite ordeal at home. It has not been easy for her to impose Zero Tolerance although she has done her best.

> 'There's quite a big age gap between the boys, nearly five years, and whilst they haven't ever fought badly, there were times when

Michael would whack Robbie just for being an annoying little brother. And, of course, with the Latin background and what went on at home, there is a certain physicality in the way they express their anger and some volatility. I've always tried to talk to them about it – not necessarily about my relationship with my husband, at least not when they were young – the violence generally went on behind closed doors and no-one wanted to think about it, although they knew what was going on – but about bullying and the dangers of hurting someone if you are violent towards them.

As they grew into teenage it became more difficult because they were bigger, tougher and more physical and I did once have a confrontation with Michael who had his hand raised to me. I said very quietly, "If you do this, you must leave the house", and it stopped. Of course, they are aware that I did take out an injunction against their father to keep him away from me, so I guess he knew I meant what I said.

As they have got older they have brought up the subject and they have said their father is a bully who tries to gain respect through fear. Michael now acknowledges that what happened was wrong, that standing and screaming in someone's face is just not the way. I don't shout because I know how hurtful it can be. It's very hard sometimes, but if they are frustrated or cross I just try to hug them out of it.'

On the whole, I think Linda is right about shouting. In March 2002 the NSPCC published research, which showed 87 per cent of parents shout at their children and it's not something of which the NSPCC approves. Indeed, some work published around the same time by psychologists in Denmark claimed that shouting at children was more likely to cause long-term psychological damage than smacking. But I also think we have to recognise that parents are human.

I worry a lot about parenting classes that urge negotiation at all times, biting your tongue and retiring to another room for time-out if you are about to lose it. It seems to me an impossible ideal to sustain and I doubt we really want our boys to think their mothers are the parental equivalent of silent and acquiescent Stepford

Wives. It's not a good idea to shower verbal abuse at children, or use the kind of language that belittles or humiliates them, but letting off steam at the top of your voice occasionally can't do harm in my view. They'll encounter it in the outside world and it's not such a bad thing to realise their parents are far from perfect.

Fighting at home can be difficult to stop once it starts, but there are ways, as Anna and Linda have demonstrated, of setting boundaries, which make it clear that it is unacceptable. Tim Kahn in *Bringing Up Boys* suggests that the physicality of boys in pushing, joshing and even scrapping with each other may occur in part because they are so frequently deprived of physical affection or they exist in an environment where it's not cool to have a cuddle. Being physically affectionate with and attentive to them may take away some of the need to roll around with each other.

I can take no credit in my house, apart from being very cuddly, for all the battles that were prevented when my two were small. The genius for distraction rested with our nanny Jeanne who could always spot a potentially explosive situation developing. It requires a huge amount of energy and inventiveness on the part of the carer, but a new game, getting out the paints, walking the dogs, helping with cooking the lunch, looking at a new book were all constantly applied diversionary tactics that averted trouble. It's essential with any boys to prevent them harming each other, but was especially so in our case because, as in Linda's family, a four-year age gap can mean the younger one is potentially physically in great danger if the murderous jealousy of an older and much bigger brother, who can't forgive the younger for being born, develops into the worst case of sibling rivalry since Cain and Abel.

It's important to teach negotiating skills within the family as the boys get older. You have to make sure a younger child knows that he's not allowed to interfere with his older brother's things or go into his room without an invitation. Equally the older boy has to respect the younger one's privacy and be aware that beating up someone small, picking a fight he will always win, is, as Anna says, bullying. It's also worth making him aware that younger children can develop a clever tactic of their own, guaranteed to get an older brother into trouble. There was a period when Charlie discovered he had power over Edward. He would poke and prod him to the point when Ed's temper would overflow, Ed would whack Charlie, Charlie would cry blue murder, I would sympathise with Charlie – younger and smaller – and Ed would get into trouble. It took me a while to work out that Charlie was doing it deliberately, and then punish them both equally. (Ed will argue I never quite mastered this one!)

I'm a great believer in setting boundaries for behaviour of all kinds – fighting, rudeness, unwillingness to co-operate – and punishing any misdemeanour. My usual tactics, which seem to work best, are withdrawal of privileges and making the punishment fit the crime. If something gets broken because of silliness or carelessness, pocket money is deducted to pay for it. If they are rude they have to make a public apology. If they fight, like Anna, I ban games or TV or, when going out became an important part of their lives, I grounded them. I learned from bitter experience of trying to make Charlie actually stay in his room and failing, not to pack him off upstairs. It does seem unfair to send the boys to their rooms as a punishment because their rooms should be comforting havens, not prison cells. I discovered the most effective way of separating them and giving everybody a chance to cool off was to send them to separate rooms or out into the garden whilst I stayed in the kitchen.

I do give them the opportunity to discuss the rules and boundaries that are set. There is no point, in today's climate, denying them the opportunity to question and challenge authority, and, if they have a reasonable defence, I will listen. Ed, for instance, once tripped and broke a precious hand-painted glass vase, which I had inherited from a great aunt and nurtured through every house move I'd ever made. He knew it was a 'kids hands off' item, but had brought me some flowers back from school and had only been trying to please me by filling up the vase with water and arranging the flowers. I listened to his argument and asked him what he thought we should do about it. He found a grotty old stoneware vase and hand-painted it himself. Its sentimental value far outweighs the actual value of the broken one.

Generally, though, I've always made it clear that we do not run a domestic democracy. A certain standard of behaviour is expected and if they are not prepared to go along with it they will be punished. 'No' means 'No' and no amount of pester power or persuasion will shift a decision once made. I do, though, always give credit when it's due. Boys do genuinely want to please their parents and reinforcing good behaviour will teach them that they're more likely to get attention if they behave well than if they behave badly.

It's also wise to point out misdemeanours in an explanatory, rather than an accusatory way. Charlie has a habit of not phoning when he's promised he will to let us know what time he will need picking up. Rather than saying, 'Why can you never make a phone call when you promised, you selfish little so and so', I've tried to explain that I'm not trying to keep tabs or make him feel like a baby, but it makes my day impossible if I'm not given adequate warning of when he's going to need me to provide a taxi service. When he does remember to call I praise him to the hills.

I don't believe in smacking. I can't put my hand on my heart and say I've never lost it and whacked them. Charlie, bless him, tried to make me feel better during a discussion in the car about one particularly volatile incident we'd been through where it's alleged I chased him through the house with an old walking stick – which, I hasten to add, I didn't actually use, but probably only because I couldn't catch him!

He was about seven at the time and told me that, whilst he took my point about how grown-ups shouldn't hit children because they don't expect to be hit themselves, he didn't think women ever deserved it, but children sometimes did. 'Women,' he opined rather wisely, 'tend not to trash their rooms' – the very offence for which I'd been so incensed. So, on rare occasions when they have been really impossible, I have lashed out, but it really doesn't work.

You feel ashamed to have been reduced to the lowest point possible and they feel angry and resentful. There is no such thing as physical chastisement delivered with love, it is always delivered in anger or frustration and, if we're trying to raise boys who have respect for those smaller and weaker than themselves, we have no moral ground to stand on if we have set an example that suggests violence against someone smaller and weaker is a way of making them do what you want them to.

One of the saddest people I've spoken to during the research for this book was a woman who I shan't name because she asked me not to. The problems she had with her son are, she thinks, now resolved as he's in his twenties and seems to have settled down with a girlfriend, but during his teens he became violent towards her. She is small in stature and even the bigger mums among us know how tall and intimidating the lads can appear when they suddenly shoot up to 6 foot 2 inches with size 13 feet, but still have the brain of a battering ram.

For her, her son became terrifying. She's been a single parent since her husband left her when her son was small and, as he hit teenage, he began to realise he could gain power over her by being verbally and physically threatening. It began with pushing and swearing and he hit her several times. She felt there was nothing she could do and merely weathered the storms, getting out of his way whenever he was 'in a mood' and losing control over his social life – although he did get on with his school work and made it to university.

Children who abuse their parents is the last domestic taboo (there's documented evidence that some girls do it, too, and the victim can occasionally be a father, but it seems to be primarily a mother/son problem and generally when there is no father around). This woman spoke about it to no-one. It's easy to imagine why. No matter how badly they behave, we still love them and want to feel proud of them. We're also reluctant to be judged a bad or failed parent.

Dr Susan Bailey is a forensic psychiatrist and chair of the Child and Adolescent Faculty at the Royal College of Psychiatrists. She says this kind of violence might occur if a child is mimicking a violent father; he could be developing autism or suffer from a learning difficulty; a small percentage might be developing a mental illness; but for others violence may be a way they have learned of getting attention. The cycle is difficult to break, she says, if the parent becomes submissive, because the boy takes on the dominant role and feels powerful. She is concerned that there is very little help for parents in this situation apart from asking that a child be taken into care or, in extreme cases, taking them to court as happened in 1998 in a celebrated case in Wilmslow where Rupert Hawes, the son of a lawyer repeatedly and ritually humiliated and beat his mother in front of his sisters.

Rupert's father said that the abuse had begun when he was at work, 'He's a big lad and my wife has nothing like his strength and stature. It is all very well saying "Talk it over", but how do you remonstrate with someone who is blowing his top. As things got worse, we did seek help, but did not get much from the medical profession, social services and other organisations. When we discussed it with friends someone suggested giving him a good thrashing, but with a strapping six-footer like Rupert it would not have been easy anyway.'

The Hawes took the right course of action in a case like this and the young man was put on probation for assault and criminal damage. He was ordered by the magistrate to attend an anger management course and told to stay away from the family home.

Wirral Council has a unique new programme to help families where children are abusive. It was set up by Jill Bennet, head of the Social Welfare Service there, who was working with families of truanting children. Several mothers broke down in front of her and showed her bruises from where they had been attacked by their sons. Jill set up discussion groups where people in similar situations could talk to each other and build up their own and each other's self-esteem. Men and women meet in separate groups while the youth service simultaneously works with the children. The parents attend the programme for twelve weeks and the aim is to help them build a new relationship with their child.

The service has had good success rates in getting children back to school and stopping the abuse, but Jill says she hasn't managed to find one reason why the boys do it. She's also careful to point out that it occurs in all sorts of families from across the social classes, and she's in the process of doing the first piece of UK research on the phenomenon. What is clear at the moment is that when the problem occurs, it tends to be hidden, which it shouldn't be. If it begins to happen to you, talk to a GP, the social services, Women's Aid, a lawyer – anyone to get the ball rolling to put a stop to it early on. A self-help group started in Wirral by parents who have been helped by Jill can be reached by e-mail at tulipgroup@hotmail.com or by post at PO Box 156, New Ferry, Wirral, CH63 9WE.

There is a fierce debate going on at the moment within pre-school circles about whether violent play and the use of guns should be banned or permitted. It's again that problem of whether we make boys feel bad about what has traditionally been seen as male behaviour or whether we accommodate and guide it. Penny Holland is a senior lecturer in early childhood education at London Metropolitan University. For her book *We Don't Play with Guns Here*, she collated research carried out in twenty centres where small children are cared for. Since she started in 1998 she says some fifty such centres have been trying out new ideas in relaxing Zero Tolerance for very young children.

Ann Longfield, chief executive of Kid's Club Network, is fundamentally opposed to any form of violent play. The two of them went head to head in the pages of *The Guardian* in to thrash out their arguments in an article headed 'Should we let children play with war toys?':

> *'Dear Ann,*
>
> *For the last twenty to thirty years, the answer to this question has been largely an unquestioned and resounding no. Zero Tolerance of any form of war, weapon and superhero play has held sway and has been adopted by many parents. This approach has an admirable pedigree, arising from both feminist and pacifist aspirations to intervene in the spiral of violence and stamp out male violence at an early age.*
>
> *This is a perspective to which I vigorously subscribed myself, both as a parent and teacher until recently. The central difficulty is that a Zero Tolerance approach simply does not work. In addition, there is no conclusive research to implicate this area of play in the development of aggressive adult behaviour. In most early years classrooms there will always be a small group of boys (rarely girls) for whom this area of play is a dominant interest, and they are not for turning. My experience has been that far from gently enticing these boys into more "worthy" areas of play, our constant negativity towards their interests only serves to erode their self-esteem, stunt their imagination and turn them into creative liars, as the weapons they construct become mobile phones, drills or hosepipes as soon as they see an adult approach.*

On the other hand, when we relax such stringent approaches and allow children to construct weapons and play out superhero scenarios, I have seen these same boys flourish imaginatively and emotionally. Their aggressive play diminishes. (I'm not talking about toy guns as purchased in toy shops as these are single purpose toys that can only be pointed and shot – they control the child's play.) With adult support, sensitive guidance and boundaries maintained around real aggression, I'd say the answer to this question should now be yes.

Dear Penny,

The reason Zero Tolerance of war or weapon play has remained for so long is because it is right. It's important not to consider children as isolated individuals. You imply that any interest developed by a child should be encouraged rather than contained, but this ignores the fact that play with war toys can lead to behaviour that dominates or intrudes on the play of other children. Those who work in childcare have to balance the needs of all the children in their care.

I disagree with you that simply because we won't always succeed in preventing children playing with guns we should abandon all our efforts. What is more important is that we, as parents and carers, help direct children towards more positive play opportunities. Zero Tolerance of war toys will not in itself produce a less violent society, but there is no reason to give up on one area where we can make a difference.

Dear Ann,

I am not advocating that we should allow children to play with manufactured toy guns. My research is concerned with children being allowed to construct weapons from play materials as props for play, and to initiate war and superhero scenarios. Concerns about the management of potentially disruptive play, which can intimidate and distract others, have been prominent in upholding Zero Tolerance.

Far from advocating a laissez faire approach, which privileges one individual at the expense of others, I'm suggesting that we engage with children's interest in this area of play and support their imaginative development so that they can move beyond media imposed scenarios while maintaining clear boundaries around aggressive and intimidating behaviour. Children in my preliminary research were allowed to point weapons at the ceiling, walls and floor, but not at each other.

For children with no other entry point to imaginative play, it seems crucial that we hold the door open for them. Once children have come through it, their imaginative play grows and aggressive play diminishes.

Dear Penny,

I'm pleased you agree with me that children should not be allowed to play with manufactured toy guns, but allowing a loophole, where they are allowed to make their own to play with, weakens the message that guns and violence are unacceptable. The central issue is the danger that children become accustomed to violent play and that this affects their development. In the wider culture of TV and computer games, violence is often linked to success.

Violent play with toy guns should not reinforce this. Instead there must be a consistent and universal message that guns and violence are unacceptable.

Children like and need consistency from the adults who care for them. As research from the Girl Guides published this week shows, children's primary role models are parents. When parents set down consistent guidelines about war play, they send a very clear value judgement that will resonate through the years as children grow up. Nurseries should reflect this consistent message from parents. To allow children to create and play with toy guns in a nursery, when they are not allowed to at home, can create doubt and uncertainty in a child's mind, muddying the development of their value system.

Dear Ann,

Zero Tolerance may have become an avoidance strategy for adults, whereby they do not have to deal in more complex ways with the experience of violence that very small children bring into *our settings. I would suggest that greater developmental damage is caused by leaving these children alone with these frightening and disturbing influences.*

The most conclusive evidence so far on the development of adult aggression shows that parental physical punishment of children and their attitudes to aggression are the most significant influences. Children are not receiving consistent messages from all parents and carers: quite the opposite. Allowing war, weapon and superhero play does not have to lead to an escalation in violent play, nor does it prevent us from tackling real aggression in a clear and consistent way. Children are far more able to discriminate between fantasy and reality than is generally assumed.

Dear Penny,

We both share the desire for children to grow up in an environment free from violence. We both want children to be free to develop their potential through play and learning. We also recognise that parents are the main influence on the development of a child's attitude to violence. But we must continue to differ fundamentally on the inclusion of war toys in play. I do not want to exclude play with war toys to satisfy my own attitude to guns, I do it because I want children to realise that violence is not a necessary or desirable part of life. Play is a child's way of coping with life and developing emotionally or intellectually, but the content of that play can sometimes reinforce harmful attitudes learnt or experienced elsewhere. Let us agree the best childcare allows children to escape from parts of their lives that cause them emotional or physical pain. Instead it helps them develop their full potential in a reassuring, secure environment free from violence or representations of violence.'

So, if you are looking for childcare in a nursery or crèche, you pays your money and you makes your choice, but it's obviously an important question to ask when you are deciding what's best for your boys. And when the experts are so fundamentally opposed it's very hard for a parent to know what's best.

Personally, I have struggled with this one for years, and have, in the end come down on Ann's side. It's important to notice that

Penny says it's only a small number of boys and some girls who insist on this kind of violent play, so it's not a 'guy' thing which infects all lads as part of their genetic make-up. I think it's also extremely significant that both experts agree that replica guns are unacceptable.

I did have them as a child, when I played out my Annie Get Your Gun fantasy and didn't turn out to be a gun-slinging serial killer, but I was persuaded against them by two men I respect who know the real consequence of guns. Anthony Stevens is now a successful businessman in Manchester, but as a young man was one of the most feared black gang leaders in Moss Side. Steven Sefi was a Royal Marine who was badly injured in the Middle East in the '70s. Both are vehemently opposed to giving a boy the sense of misplaced power that the feel of a 'real' gun puts into their hands. Interesting that men who really know about these things don't glory in the potency and phallic qualities of 'boys toys' in the way that armchair generals and journalists insist upon doing during coverage of war.

I made the mistake of relaxing the no guns rule I had imposed on Ed, influenced by arguments suggesting that, if you don't give in, they'll use sticks, clothes pegs or whatever comes to hand. At one point Charlie had collected a veritable arsenal of weaponry and was much more dismissive about the dangers of 'carrying' than Ed has ever been. We were also living in an environment in the countryside where guns are much more an acceptable part of everyday use than would be the case in the city. It's taken some long hard discussions to persuade Charlie not to take up shooting. I would not buy toy or replica guns again or allow them into the house.

Other forms of violent play are also dangerous and difficult to control. I lived through the passion in the late '80s and early '90s for Ninja Turtles – no guns, just 'heroes in a half shell' with extraordinary skills in the martial arts. The sight of small boys yelling 'Ha so!' and taking vicious running, kicking jumps at each other was far from amusing and justified the need for a First Aid kit in the kitchen. Whilst Penny may have some justification for her argument for violent play if confined to the best run nurseries, where staff can be constantly vigilant in directing, controlling and discussing the possible consequences of violence, it's a rare parent who has the time or energy to be on top of what's going on all the time. Better to ban it than have a car that knows its own way to the local casualty department.

Most of the other parents I spoke to have learned through experience that limiting exposure to violence, both real and fictional, and being consistent about the fact that it's not acceptable either at home or school is really the only way to get the message across, although India was a little more relaxed than I feel I should have been about replica weapons.

'I tried with Oscar to avoid guns, in fact, sweetly, I tried for non-gender specific, politically correct toys at all times, so the poor child at one time had an embarrassment of brown dollies. There was absolutely no point in doing this. He used twigs, rolled up paper, pencils and his own fingers as guns and stared disgustedly at the dolls (teddies are a different thing altogether – he loves them, especially a monkey called George). By the time Archie came along I didn't care so much. We have one gun in the house, which I bought as a present in Arizona, but which doesn't fire the pellets it's supposed to because I removed them!

Of course, as soon as the gun appeared, they played with it obsessively for two weeks and then put it away and it hasn't been seen since. They had wooden shields when they were younger, which they loved and which I didn't remotely mind.

On other forms of violence I'm really not keen. Their father is more at ease than I am – he took them to see Lord of the Rings, for instance, and I wouldn't have. He is of the opinion that fantasy violence involving Orcs is one thing, and urban bloodletting in a more realistic film is another. I kind of lump them together. I hate it. If I could have my way we'd only watch nature programmes and It's A Wonderful Life. Computer games are the absolute bee in my bonnet. I monitor all of them and ban anything grotesque outright. It's non-negotiable. We have a GameCube, which seems to come with rather sweet games. This doesn't stop them from playing horrible games at other people's houses, but when that happens I swoop down and deliver terrible raging lectures to the friends' poor parents. I would genuinely *prefer my children to watch porn than to play some of the games around.'*

Both Diane Abbott and Jackie Kay have to contend with the fact that their sons are attracted by the black culture of which they are a part and by society's attitudes to young black men. Jackie says,

> *'TV can be a drag and films, because he likes these gansta rap movies. And they are problematic. But he watches a whole range of films, even foreign ones, when I get them and he comes with me to the theatre and poetry reading, so I don't feel that all the cultural influences are horrific.'*

Diane too tries to balance the influences on her son, but gets infuriated by the assumptions that are made about him.

> *'I've been very clear that there will be no guns and no violence at home, but growing up a black boy gives an extra dimension. Society is very threatened by black men so it's difficult as a parent to know how to encourage him to be his own person, strong, confident and powerful, able to assert himself and stand up for himself, and at the same time protect him from a world that will see a physically boisterous black boy as a threat.*
>
> *I'm always meticulous about advising him never to fight and never to hit back, because in a white boy it might be seen as high spirits, in a black boy it'll be seen as aggression. I remember once being in a friend's house where the children were having a party. I was sitting just around the corner of the kitchen – it was a typical North London environment – lots of white Yuppies around and my son was sitting quietly on the floor playing with the others. One of the fathers came in and didn't see me at the other end of the kitchen table. He said to my friend, "There's a little troublemaker".*
>
> *I was furious, but what can you do when those kind of attitudes exist among the white, educated middle class. As I've said, it all became very worrying when he went to junior school – it hadn't been a problem at all at his collaborative little nursery, but the playground at the new school was like World War Three. He had to*

adopt a 'cool' persona to survive. Everything he'd learned at home
about being kind and gentle gave him no kudos among his peers.
I guess I've just had to accept that the child will have two person-
alities – the one he shows to the outside world and the one who's at
home. And I just have to keep reminding him, making it clear, that
violence is dangerous for him and for other people.'

Jenny Stephen is a great believer, like her husband, in giving boys
plenty of outlets for their energy from a very young age.

'When the boys were little we lived in a house attached to a
boarding school and it had a long gallery, so even when it was
raining outside they had somewhere to run, jump, ride their trikes
and roll their balls. Outside I made sure there were plenty of activ-
ities – a water butt, a sandpit, a paddling pool and I didn't over
supervise them or worry about how dirty or messy they got. I
remember Henry once being naked in the sandpit whilst the others
fed him worms and sand. He didn't seem to mind and he came to
no harm.

I wasn't the sort of mum who worried about these things. If you
are fastidious I can imagine having boys would be jolly difficult. I
can't ever remember having to sort out a fight, they were never
particularly angry, never smashed the house. The only concession I
made to them was to clear the bottom shelves so that things didn't
get broken or spoiled and let them put their own books there and I
remember once one of the older boys pushing the swing with Henry
on it too hard. That was potentially dangerous and I had to stop it,
but that's about it.'

Professor Lynne Segal was the most sanguine about violence, but,
of course her boy is now thirty-three, so he was raised in a period
before TV and video games brought constant images of death and
destruction into the home and before Tarantino with *Pulp Fiction*
and Guy Ritchie with *Snatch* and *Lock, Stock and Two Smoking*
Barrels produced films which made boyhood heroes out of the most
appallingly violent, but funny gangsters.

'I was not particularly troubled by violence. I knew my son was not violent, he had not a single active role model for this and he had never been treated with a shred of violence in any way. Violence was just not there in his habitat or most intimate life, though of course it was certainly in the school playground, on telly and it was something he and his male buddies all feared and hated. Of course they played with guns, but I knew guns, videos etc. have no power to turn a person raised with gentleness as the fabric of their life into a violent person. The idea is fundamentally misguided in my view.'

This assertion can, I think, now be disputed as a result of the proliferation of violent images on TV, on video games and films and, of course, in the musical culture of rap. Martin Stephen, in his professional capacity as a head teacher, worries a lot about boys picking up violent messages without guidance and discussion – he says we would be very foolish not to recognise that media representations can have an effect.

'The nightmare is how television has changed. Boys' play can be hugely imitative and when the boys are copying something like WWF wrestling the mood can swiftly change and all hell can break loose. In the fourteen years I have been a head I have seen the capacity for children (both boys and girls, but particularly boys) to act violently increase. I think this is a result of how the amount of "incidental and legacy free violence" we see in popular culture has grown. I don't believe violence in popular culture is anything new, but I do think today's children see more of it in graphic form and so it is all the more important that they have rules about action and consequence pressed upon them from an early age.

What we try to teach boys is that the minute you let loose you are no longer in control over the end result. Even if you are just "play-fighting" in a school with sharp corners, desks and stairs etc. – or in the home or garden – you can end up causing real harm. And, of the course, the same is equally true if you let loose in anger. These days children have far less of an idea about either the legal or physical consequences there may be from letting loose.'

Recent research backs up Martin's assertion that violence in popular culture can influence behaviour. A British study found that the amount of violence on TV had doubled in two years. Viewers watched as many as 335 characters die violently in a fourteen-day period. Earlier this year the University of Michigan published persuasive evidence of cause and effect as a result of a study begun in the '70s of a group of 329 six to ten year olds in Chicago.

The team led by Dr Rowell Huesman followed up on work carried out by psychologists in the original work, which had identified the degree to which children were drawn to the violent programmes they most liked, the degree to which they identified with the most aggressive characters and how realistic they thought the characters were. Examples of shows that were rated as very violent were *Starsky and Hutch*, *The Six Million Dollar Man* and the *Roadrunner* cartoons.

The original boys and girls who are now in their early thirties were asked about their favourite programmes as adults and about aggressive behaviour. Their level of aggression was also rated by spouses or friends and checked against criminal records and traffic offences. The results showed that men who had watched a high proportion of violent programmes as children were three times more likely to have pushed, grabbed and shoved their spouses, responded violently to an insult or been convicted of a criminal offence. Women who had watched a lot of violent TV as children were four times more likely to have thrown something at their partners, hit someone who had made them angry or to have committed a criminal or traffic offence.

Personally I haven't banned games such as Grand Theft Auto, CD's with 'Parental Advisory' lyrics or videos of the most popular movies such as *Lock, Stock* from the house. Like India I was only too aware that the children would have access to them in other people's houses and I prefer to be aware of what they are watching and hearing so that I can always put in my two penn'orth of discussion to at least make them think about what messages they are absorbing.

As I was writing this section they both came into my room to look over my shoulder. I had some notes on some of the worst rap lyrics they've brought into the house (e.g. Snoop Doggy Dog: 'Cup of that Gin and Juice, I blank a bitch out, then turn the bitch out, look here there ain't no need for you to be wasting my time, see I picked you up, now I'm gonna stick you up, and dick you up!'). I was treated to a short concert demonstrating that they knew the words by heart to all these songs, a political lecture on the marginalisation of young black men and their 'justifiable' anger at racist police and an admission that the attitude to 'bitches' and 'hos' expressed in the music is totally unacceptable. So my messages about this kind of music – that, like sexist and racist jokes, it brutalises and normalises violence – must have hit home at some point.

One of the most interesting and illuminating pieces of research I came across in the writing of this book dropped into my ears one Sunday morning when I was lying in bed, listening to the radio, as a diversionary tactic from having to sit down and get on with writing. Lots of us have noticed that a meal of burgers, chips, white bread, ketchup, ice cream with chocolate sauce and coke will send a child into a flat spin of manic energy, followed by a dull slump or that a packet of highly coloured sweets will induce a couple of hours lunacy. There's now strong scientific evidence to back up what we suspected all along.

In 2003, Radio 4's *The Food Programme* posed the following questions,

> *'We know that what we eat is what we are, but what about, "I eat, therefore I think?" What can food do for your happiness, your mental health and your aggression levels? Could a better diet help reduce suicides and anti-social behaviour among young offenders? If so what could it do for school children, frustrated commuters, stressed employees and the rest of us? Are we ignoring one of the easiest ways to improve our behaviour and thus our lives?'*

First they attended a 'Brain Food' dinner at the School of Biological Sciences at the University of Surrey in Guildford, where Dr Margaret Rayman had arranged the event for MSc students, some of whom were doctors. On the menu were:

Canapés

Mushroom (Cu, Zn, Se, B vitamins except B12) and pine nuts (n-3 PUFA, Fe, Zn, Se, Cu, Mn)
Cherry tomatoes with smoked mackerel filling (n-2 LCPUFA, Se, I, Cu)
chicken liver pâté (B vitamins, Fe, Zn, Cu, Mn)
trout mousse with anchovy (n-3 LCPUFA, B vitamins, Se, I, Fe)

Starter

Chicken liver pâté (as above) with exotic green salad (folate, Mg)
Or
Eggs florentine (poached egg – Fe, B12, B6, folate) on a bed of spinach (folate, beta carotene, Mg) with béchamel and cheese sauce (Fe, B12, I)
Served with linseed and brazil nut toast and rolls (n-3 PUFA, Se, vitamin E, B vitamins, Cr, Zn, Si, Cu)

Main course

Citrus salmon (n-3 LCPUFA, B12, B6, vitamin C, Se, I, Cu)
Or
Baked aubergines with peppers and walnuts (n-3 PUFA, beta carotene, vitamin C and some B vitamins)
New potatoes (vitamin C)
Broccoli, spinach and ratatouille (beta carotene, folate and other B vitamins, vitamin C, Mg)

Pudding

Chocolate (Fe) tart with raspberry coulis (vitamin C)
Or
Summer fruit salad (vitamin C and other vitamins)
Both served with fresh cream or yoghurt (Fe, B12, I)

Petit fours

Chocolate brazils (Se, Fe), chocolate raisins (Mg, Fe, Cu, B6)

Guide to symbols
Cu – Copper
Zn – Zinc
PUFA – polyunsaturated fatty acids (LU-long chain)
Fe – Iron
Se – Selenium
Mn – Manganese
Cr – Chromium
Si – Silicone
I – Iodine
Mg – Magnesium

Dr Rayman advocates this kind of diet for anyone who needs to have a sharp mind – she describes it as an 'intellectually uplifting menu', but she also emphasises how good it is for teenagers especially to eat this type of food with the range of minerals and fatty acids it contains.

'All the fish – the smoked mackerel and the salmon – are rich in Omega 3 fatty acids. The pine nuts are a good substitute for vegetarians or people who don't like fish. They are important in the treatment of schizophrenia and depression, so are necessary in the regular diet in significant quantities.

The eggs contain B12 and iron and these are very important for teenagers. If they become iron deficient they can be unstable and forgetful. The spinach doesn't provide iron, although we were led to believe in the past it does. It does contain folate though which is also important to the brain. The linseed, brazil nut and wholemeal bread contains Omega 3 again and Selenium which is very necessary for cognitive function. The surprising thing to me in holding this event is how few of the GPs here are aware of the link between food and the brain.'

The programme also looked at an experiment conducted at Aylesbury's Centre for young Offenders where Dr Bernard Gesh and his organisation Natural Justice carried out a blind test on the inmates, described by the Deputy Governor, Trevor Hussey, as 'very violent. Some of them have been sent down for life and we have had a high level of assaults on staff and other inmates'.

In the trial, half the young men were given supplements containing multi-vitamins, minerals and fatty acids. The other group was given a placebo. The diet was found to be OK, but as Trevor Hussey explained, it's always difficult in a prison environment to give prisoners food they want to eat that's also good for them, so there tends to be an overemphasis on carbohydrates, fats and sugars.

The results of the study were startling. There was a 35 per cent drop in violent incidents and it was clear that no other factors were involved apart from the dietary supplements. The two groups were clearly defined and the reduction in violence and other offending behaviour had only occurred in the group taking the supplements. Nevertheless, the Home Office has refused to fund any further research. The former Chief Inspector of Prisons, Sir David Ramsbotham, finds this quite extraordinary.

'This trial is beyond dispute. It is 92 per cent statistically proven which is totally convincing. Proper diet is the basis of good behaviour and this has much wider implications. Tony Blair has said he wants to be "Tough on the causes of crime". If bad nutrition is one of the causes of crime we should be improving the diet right now at home and at school.'

We can all start at home and begin to campaign to persuade schools to pay more attention to the quality of children's diet. Removing vending machines which encourage over-consumption of sugary drinks, sweets and chocolates, common in many secondary schools, would be a start. If the research is as good as the experts claim, it could bring about a revolution in violent behaviour and save us all a lot of worry and grief.

CHAPTER SIX

SCHOOLBOYS

'Girls outperform boys', 'Failing boys', 'What's wrong with boys?' 'Boys swagger whilst girls win prizes', 'Boys are tomorrow's second sex', 'Girls outnumber boys at medical and veterinary schools', 'Girls are succeeding at the expense of boys', 'Boys are struggling', 'Boys are in deep trouble'. If you were to believe the headlines you'd think the feminist revolution had been fought and won, women were now running the world and a generation of emasculated males was limping along behind them, weeping into a sea of lager. The received wisdom, emblazoned regularly across the newspapers, says that 54 per cent of girls get five or more top A to C grade passes compared with 45 per cent of boys. So let's set this into perspective.

First, none of this anxiety about boys in new. In 1693 the English philosopher, John Locke, wrote in his treatise, *Some Thoughts Concerning Education*, that schools were failing to develop 'writing and speaking skills in young gentlemen'. (No need to blame girls in those days, of course; they were generally considered unworthy of any education except at home, if their class allowed it, in reading and music, needlework and running a household!) The public schools of early nineteenth-century Victorian England were expected to promote 'acceptable codes of manliness' and make men into 'tough, decisive, courageous leaders'. Thus, as Christine Skelton points out in *Schooling the Boys*:

'Ideas that schools are failing boys and that they construct and/or

can challenge particular dominant images of masculinity obviously
have a long history and are not phenomena of recent times.'

Nor should it surprise us if girls are slightly (and it is slightly and
only in some subjects) ahead of the game. It was ever thus. Once
girls finally won themselves the right to a free and universal education alongside the boys in the '40s and '50s, they were found to
perform slightly better in the 11 Plus, which gave access to
grammar school education to those who passed. So gender quotas
were imposed which lasted in some parts of the country until the
late 1980s, when the Equal Opportunities Commission took
Northern Ireland's Department of Education and Birmingham City
Council to court to end the discriminatory practice.

This unfair selection was first made public in 1954 when a magazine called *The Hunts Post* ran the headline 'Girls brainier than
boys'. It informed its readers that too many girls had been passing
the 11 Plus, so education authorities all over Britain had decided to
limit numbers of girls going to grammar school. For all those years,
some of the girls who had passed the 11 Plus were sent to secondary
modern, rather than grammar schools, while boys with lower marks
went to grammar schools instead. It's estimated that without the
male quota in mixed grammar schools, two-thirds of every classroom would have been occupied by girls.

One reason put forward for the imposition of specific quotas of
boys attending grammar school was that they were supposedly late
developers (there's no reliable evidence for this at all – see later in
this chapter) and, to accommodate their later and greater potential, more places in better educational establishments were to be
reserved for them. The other possible explanation, and the more
likely, was the post-war push to return women to the home. Men
coming back from the war were to be given the jobs women had
occupied during the war years, and the nurseries, which had
accommodated their children, closed virtually overnight.

Encouraging women to return to the kitchen was reflected in the
school curriculum and dictated the kind of education boys and girls
could expect to receive. Boys were to be prepared for the world of
work whilst girls' education would emphasise sewing, cooking and,

as my mother recalled, although I had wiped it out of my mind, how to scrub a deal table and how to starch and press a collar and cuffs. (And I went to grammar school!)

There's no doubt that there was a need for changes in the opportunities offered to girls in order to encourage them to recognise that they too could do maths, physics, chemistry and metalwork, not just domestic science and the arts. As late as 1971 a teacher called Jo O'Brien, who was interviewed on *Woman's Hour*, said,

> *'It isn't difficult to be specific about inequalities when you consider that only 6 per cent of all British apprentices are female, that three times as many girls as boys leave school at fifteen and that only 28 per cent of university students are female in this country (a rise of only 1 per cent since 1966). As a teacher I find that at sixteen, which is the age I teach, you realise girls have been very influenced by what is expected of them in this society. They think their role is to sit inside the classroom quietly applauding the boys. This damages their capacity to learn, their capacity to develop as people. What we want is an education where, if girls wish to, they can become metal welders and the implication of that is that men, if they want to become ballet dancers, can do so without there being any question of it being challenged.'*

I think we often forget in this debate about whether girls have been given too much help and an unfair advantage over boys, that the widening of girls' choices and a commitment to true equality can, when correctly handled, broaden opportunities for boys as well.

It's generally agreed in current serious academic works that the new emphasis in the press on boys 'underachievement' and the consequent rush to address it in political and educational circles comes as a result of what Skelton describes in her study as being 'largely due to a superficial reading of the statistics'. She explains that it is only recently that government agencies have collected these kinds of data, since the introduction of league tables and parents' reliance on them to make a choice of school for their child. Skelton goes on to say:

'Even with more detailed evidence, the data that are made public are not specific enough for adequate comparisons to be made. The absence of sophisticated data sets has not prevented conclusions being reached on the basis of statistical information. It should be reiterated that media hyperbole has led to a distorted impression that boys' underachievement refers to all boys and is widespread across schools. The boys' underachievement debate as reported in the majority of the media is over-exaggerated and misinformed.'

In *What About the Boys – Issues of Masculinity in Schools*, the authors survey a wealth of academic research in this country and in Australia on the so-called gender gap in education and reach similar conclusions:

'This literature demonstrates that there is very little common ground between academic research and populist discussions of gender differences in schooling and its outcomes. In the new populist discourse, male failure in education is posited as a corollary of female success. Although there is little evidence that girls' improvement in examinations has been at the expense of boys, the predominant gender discourse in the mid-1990s is that of male underachievement.

While media statements such as "girls are out-performing boys" have become commonplace in both Australia and the UK, they are inaccurate in several ways. First, they confuse performance or measured achievement with participation – that is, the number and composition of students. Second they ignore the question of the inequities in post-school rewards for girls for the same or better achievement at school. These claims are typically based on the outstanding achievements of a small, select group of girls, not representative of the diverse female population, and ignore complex within-gender differences for both boys and girls. More important, they obscure the crucial point that, to date, girls' school achievement has had no positive impact on post-school career prospects for them.

Furthermore, recent Australian research shows that gender differences have emerged in students' use of schooling as a credential, and in post-school rewards, where girls are faring worse than boys for the

*same or better achievement than them. The populist climate which
sees boys as the new disadvantaged has obscured, first, the fact that
there is no clear nexus between school achievement and post-school
pathways for girls in the way that there is for boys, and, second, the
question of why these pathways remain so restrictive and limiting for
girls, including the high achievers.'*

This point has been acknowledged in Britain. In November 2002
David Bell, the head of the Government's education standards
body, Ofsted, in an address to head teachers warned against
concentrating too hard on narrowing the apparent gap between
the performance of girls and boys, but said schools should still be
concerned about how well girls were doing. Mr Bell told the
conference:

*'There is strong evidence that girls need to do better than boys if
they are to gain the benefits that are properly theirs. The relative
weaknesses in boys' performance have stolen all the headlines in
recent times. It could look as if we weren't really worried about the
girls. There have been some real successes in terms of girls' participation in maths, science, design and information technology in
recent years. Nevertheless I still think we should continue to be
concerned about how well girls are doing.*

*Research from the Organisation for Economic Co-operation
and Development shows that the gender gap in terms of getting jobs
is only half as much for women with university qualifications as it
is for those with lesser qualifications. This shows there is an added
benefit from the trend of more girls going into higher education. But
the achievement of girls continues to be a matter of pressing
concern if girls are to overcome some of the disadvantages that are
still inherent in the economy.'*

Recent research from the Equal Opportunities Commission (EOC)
bears out the apparent disadvantage suffered by girls and women
once they leave school. The data suggests that a woman who
continued in employment throughout her life could expect to earn
£250,000 less than a man in similar position. The study also shows

that more men were being appointed to top jobs in industry, and even to the headships of schools, despite the fact that women were getting degrees which were just as good as their male counterparts.

Further studies by the Institute for Employment Studies show that women are still being paid almost a fifth less than men. The gap in average pay is 19 per cent. This can partly be attributed to the fact that a higher proportion of women work in traditionally less well paid jobs, such as nursing, catering, sales and services, but the EOC has shown that the pay gap affects also women graduates, exploding the myth that it is caused by a lack of education among women. Female graduates earn an average of £13.22 per hour, whilst male graduates get an average hourly rate of £16.38. Indeed one male veterinary student of my acquaintance told me he had been reassured by his tutors that he would be certain to have his pick of the most satisfying and best paid jobs in the industry because of his gender, this despite the fact that the vet schools are now training many more women than men.

Much has been made of the fact that medical and veterinary schools are now taking more girls than boys – in some colleges students are between 60 and 90 per cent female. This, naturally, has been characterised as further evidence that girls are doing better than boys and that boys are being excluded from some of our most respected professions. I spoke to two senior figures in academia to find out what was really going on.

Professor Lance Lanyon is head of the Royal Veterinary College in London where they have in some years had up to a 98 per cent female intake. It is, he says, a worldwide phenomenon. Before the war the profession was almost entirely male; in the '60s, a quota was imposed to ensure a 10 per cent female intake. In the '70s it was moving towards 50/50 and now the profession is predominantly female. These figures, he says, have nothing to do with girls' greater academic success. Rather, intake is based more or less on the proportion of girls and boys applying, and Lanyon finds no difference academically in the abilities or qualifications of the sexes. The girls, he says, are marginally more mature at 18 and perform slightly better at interview, although the college allows for this difference and tries to avoid any kind of gender bias.

The dramatic shift in the gender of those applying Lanyon puts down to the change in the nature of the perception of the profession:

> 'It used to be about agriculture and large animals, so vets were seen as big, strong, prepared to get dirty and deal with hard-headed farmers and think about hard economics, not sentimentality. In recent years, through TV programmes like Vet School and Animal Hospital, it's been projected as a caring profession, concerned with the soft and furries. So girls are attracted and fewer boys are. We would definitely prefer 50/50, but we have to take what we get.'

Similarly, Dr Brenda Cross, Sub-Dean of Admissions at University College, London's Medical School, where the intake is now 60/40 in favour of girls, says that the college, too, is admitting students purely in the proportion in which they apply. Academically, she says, there is no discernible difference between the two sexes, although, again, girls perform slightly better than boys in their interviews and written statements. She, like Professor Lanyon, is convinced that it's the changing image of the profession that's making it increasingly unattractive to young males:

> 'It's seen as a caring profession which demands long hours and relatively poor remuneration. I think the boys want easier lives and they are looking towards more valued professions in which they are paid well. I don't mind if you quote me on this, because things are becoming dangerously unbalanced. We know from what happened in the Soviet Union, and it applies here to teaching and nursing, that if a profession starts to be seen as 'women's work' it gets downgraded in society's eyes. To be honest with you, we are desperate for more males, particularly white Caucasian males.'

So, yet again, the popular perception that boys are useless and failing is not borne out in practice, although the experience of both these academics at the coal face does suggest that training for boys in how to conduct and project themselves at interview might be useful, given that the culture they inhabit frequently mitigates against them honing their literary and conversational skills, particularly if they have chosen to study science. I did this with Ed, sending him off to friends with experience of interviewing to learn how to sell himself and what sort of questions to expect. It seems boys are less confident about showing off their talents than girls – it's one of those things they see as uncool.

So, if boys are not going for medical and veterinary science any more, what are the 'more valued and better paid professions' in which they are interested? At one all-boys' school in 2002 the list of school leavers who went on to higher and further education shows a clear predominance of boys choosing to study economics, business, finance, computer science, engineering, politics and law – all seen to lead to high-status, well-paid and well-respected careers.

It seems obvious to me from all this evidence that the hysterical and misleading reactions in the press to the supposed failure of boys in relation to girls are nothing more than a manifestation of the backlash which has greeted every advancement of women and girls since the women's movement began. It serves no useful purpose other than to draw ever more divisive battle lines in the sex war when we should all be working towards peace negotiations.

None of this should suggest that there are not problems and concerns that should be addressed in order to improve the education of both boys and girls in schools and particularly their understanding of each other and the constraints gender stereotyping can place upon them. Christine Skelton in her research on primary schools demonstrates how children are quickly made aware of gender differences and of 'male superiority', no matter how hard the school has tried to remove any literature that smacks of outdated sexism.

Even small boys and girls immediately have separate toilets, changing rooms and play areas – and sadly, still, it's football that dominates the recreational spaces. She also observes it's the noisiest and pushiest boys who tend to dominate the teacher's attention in the classroom. This emphasis on difference, the message that being pushy gets attention and an excess of respect for those with sporting prowess disadvantages not only the less bouncy girls, but also the quieter, more studious boys who are invariably branded by their peers as uncool.

It's often argued that more male teachers in primary schools would help in 'controlling' boys' over enthusiasm or lack of respect for the quiet atmosphere required for a learning environment. Skelton sees danger in this approach, as male teachers are more likely to have responsibility for the high-status areas of the curriculum, such as maths and science, to occupy the most senior positions in the schools and to be seen as responsible for 'discipline'.

It's interesting that Martin Stephen, in his capacity as High Master of Manchester Grammar School, saw as a priority on his arrival at the school nearly ten years ago the introduction of more women teachers in the 'high-status' subjects such as maths and science, so that, even in a highly academic all-boys school, the boys were not given the impression that it's only men who can function brilliantly in these areas. It's worth remarking that Martin is strongly influenced in his views on how to achieve better gender understanding among the boys in his school by the fact that he and his wife Jenny have had dual careers in teaching whilst bringing up their three sons.

In her study of one particular primary school, Deneway, situated in a middle class area of Oldchester, Skelton notes how little we have considered the question I've looked at in other parts of this book, 'What kind of male role models/teachers do we want our boys to be exposed to?' Of the fourteen teaching staff at the school three were male. Equality of opportunity was frequently referred to in the school's brochure and this commitment was supported by curriculum activities:

'A Year 6 class undertook a topic on gender which involved the pupils in a range of activities such as carrying out an observational study at the local Tesco's to see who did the shopping, while one of the girls compiled a questionnaire for teachers to answer which attempted to find out their knowledge of 'women in society'. Added to this curriculum opportunities were provided for co-operative games, knitting sewing and cooking for all pupils. Furthermore, the men teachers would refer to gender equality with pupils and teachers. For example, on one occasion the school secretary came into a Year 5 class and asked for two strong boys to help move some *classroom furniture. To which Philip Norris responded, "We have strong girls here too". However an outward support for equality did not tackle the subtle ways in which gender relational practices actively privileged a particular form of masculinity to which the men teachers aligned themselves.'*

This Skelton describes as being a 'middle class, adult male version of "the lads"'. It was shown particularly in the role of humour in classroom management and in the central role football played in the school. The list of extra curricular activities in the school was listed in order of priority:

> *Football*
> *Rugby*
> *Athletics/cross country*
> *Dance*
> *Nature Club*
> *Cooking*
> *Recorders etc.*

Football, for which the school had developed a strong reputation, was ring fenced as an exclusively male competitive sport. The school team was all male, the coaches were male and 'it was unusual not to see the men teachers, Philip Norris in particular, having a "kick around" with the boys on the playground or the school field at lunchtime'. Skelton also demonstrates the way in which the language used between the male teachers and sporty boys was often coded, indicating these boys' superiority over those from other schools and to exclude the girls and less sporty boys.

When girls were allowed to join in football during PE lessons the male class teachers used it as an opportunity to give the boys more practice. The girls were always asked if they wanted to join in, but it was not assumed that everyone would have a go, and most refused. Those girls and some of the boys, who did join in, were disadvantaged by the accepted forms of communication, such as being given masculine nicknames. One girl, Hilary, who was named Thumper, was observed to freeze every time her nickname was used. Another was called Lanky and Skelton concludes that it's fair to surmise that, as pre-adolescent girls, they were sensitive to the physical changes they were going through and did not want attention drawn to any part of their bodies. Several of the girls talked about how the male teachers made them very aware that football was something they were not supposed to take part in.

One teacher in particular made jokes about non-sexist language in the classroom.

'I have a friend who thought his name was sexist so he changed it. He used to be called Guy Chapman and now he's Person Personperson.'

This same teacher made cracks about the use of Ms, deliberately used the word 'ladies' when the class had been discussing whether 'women' was a more appropriate term and at the end of the lesson called back two boys in front of the whole class and said,

'Gentlemen! Come back here and tidy this table for me. It has to be a gentleman . . . we can't ask the girls can we?'

Is it any wonder that boys embrace a laddish culture in which they undermine girls – make jokes about them and anything they do, such as reading, working co-operatively or studying quietly as uncool – if their male role models, even their teachers, openly subvert the serious messages offered by feminism on how to move towards gender equality by sending them up? Skelton puts forward a strong argument for male teachers to be given training, which addresses the subtle messages they may be giving out.

Teachers also need to learn that becoming 'matey' or 'laddish' with some of the boys in their care may well be good for some, but could disadvantage other types of boys. Christine Skelton also questions one of the arguments put forward for having male teachers in the school – that they will counterbalance what's assumed to be the softer, feminine approach of female teachers and which, it's said, gives girls an advantage. It is, she contends, ludicrous:

'For one thing, the idea that we might be arguing for more male nurses to counterbalance a female dominated profession on the basis that men can offer "tough love" and "sternness"' to male

patients sounds ridiculous. It is enough to say that it is clearly preferable for children to see adults working across a range of occupations.'

Equally, female teachers need extra training to ensure that any baggage they carry around as women – 'all men are bastards, faithless, troublesome, lazy', all the things women regularly trot out when they talk about men – does not mitigate against boisterous or less able boys.

Clare Wigzell and her partner have three boys and live in Leeds. Clare has spent her working life in education. George is eighteen and a high flier; Elliott is fifteen and the least academically gifted of the three; Will at eight and a half seems to be developing in much the same way as his eldest brother. The two older boys attend the same mixed comprehensive, but their experiences at school could not be more different.

George always got on with his work and had no worries about being perceived as a swot. Elliott thinks being a swot is uncool, struggles to achieve the national average in SATS and other tests and basically conforms to the stereotype of the 'failing boy'. There seems to be no doubt that he suffers from teachers' assumptions about him. His mother describes it thus:

'It seems to be a vicious circle. His lack of ease at his studies and difficulties with language and reading have made him a rather terse, blunt speaker. He is continually misread. For instance if Elliott hasn't done a task he's supposed to have done, the first question is not, why hasn't he done it, he must be in difficulty. It's assumed he's lazy and insolent. We see a young man struggling, but the teachers seem to treat him as a young man with "a reputation and attitude".

He does have a strong sense of himself and is confident in his artistic talents, so he probably does get a bit disrespectful, possibly even a bit aggressive with teachers. He doesn't take any bullshit. But I've felt all along that they've looked at him, jumped to the conclusion that he's not clever and studious like his older brother and written him off.

We've had him tested to see if there are any serious underlying learning difficulties and nothing was uncovered. His argument is that he's in the same band as a third of all kids, so what's the bother if he's not really interested in the National Curriculum and reading and all that stuff. We, of course, worry about him terribly. We feel we've failed as parents and he may not get the qualifications he needs for a good job, but the system doesn't seem to serve boys like Elliott well.

The National Curriculum is too word based for the boys (and girls) who don't have reading in their background or who, like Elliott, just don't have a talent for language and I'm quite sure that whilst a "failing" girl is probably left to fester quietly in a corner, a "failing" boy is expected to be trouble and treated accordingly. If they are expected to be bad, they'll live up to it. And what may be seen as a bit of cheek or even assertiveness in a girl is read as aggression in a boy. He was suspended twice before Christmas for being "disrespectful".'

Clare's theory about different attitudes of teachers to boys and girls and the different behaviour patterns into which boys and girls are socialised is borne out in interesting new research on Attention Deficit Hyperactivity Disorder (ADHD). The work was carried out in Sweden by Svenny Kopp who's a child psychiatrist at the University of Gothenburg. The ADHD figures there are similar to those in this country. Five per cent of children here are estimated to have some form of the disorder – some 370,000 children under sixteen. It's always been assumed more boys suffer from it than girls, but girls already make up about a third of the number. What Kopp's work has shown is that girls are severely under diagnosed and there may be many more of them who suffer from the condition than we have thus far assumed.

Dr Nikos Mytas, a consultant child and adolescent psychiatrist in North London says the effects of gender conditioning are the root cause of under diagnosis in girls. Mytas and Kopp agree that the symptoms, the same for both girls and boys, are extreme – failing to listen, poor organisation, being easily distracted, not completing tasks, always forgetting necessary items, being overactive, squirming, fidgeting, wandering, running, never walking, climbing on everything, swinging from the light fittings, failing to wait their turn, interrupting with irrelevancies, not holding back, playing noisily, being uncontrollable under any circumstances. But the boys display the loud and noisy behaviour at home, at school and in the clinic; girls by contrast, are every bit as bad at home, but at school and, if they ever get referred to the clinic, just tend to daydream. One mother told me it took her months to finally persuade the doctors at the clinic that her daughter was completely different at home; finally she got her diagnosis.

Dr Mytas believes the reason for this difference in girls' behaviour outside is clear. Boys are socialised into being given permission to misbehave (boys will be boys), so the relatively small number who do suffer from ADHD have no shame in being seen as 'naughty, difficult or uncontrollable' at home and in public. By contrast, the girls, he says, are so conditioned into behaving themselves when outside the home that they internalise their mental difficulties and turn in on themselves. Mytas worries about their under diagnosis, as there might be hundreds of women believing they are depressive or manic depressive simply because they have not had their ADHD identified and treated.

I have, by the way, only included this research on ADHD, as it offers such a clear example of how gender affects the way children's behaviour is determined and perceived. As I've shown, the number of sufferers is relatively low and, in boys at least, symptoms are generally clearly beyond what would be considered normally boisterous. Parents and teachers alike should easily identify them, and referral and diagnosis should be easy to come by. But please don't assume that a normal bouncy, boisterous, energetic lad needs Ritalin to calm him down.

How, then, do we begin to resolve some of the problems that do exist in educating both boys and girls in an environment that is conducive to learning for both sexes? Steve Biddulph in *Raising Boys* offers anecdotal evidence for his assertion that boys, by the time they reach six or seven (the stage at which they begin 'serious schooling'), are six to twelve months less developed mentally than girls and should consequently be held back.

> '*In talking to heads of infant departments (from country schools in outback Australia to big international schools in Europe and Asia) the same message comes through: Boys should stay back a year. In early primary school, boys (whose motor nerves are still growing) actually get signals from their body saying, Move around, use me. To a stressed out teacher, this looks like misbehaviour. A boy sees that his craft work, drawing and writing are not as good as the girls' and thinks, "This is not for me." He quickly switches off from learning – especially if there is not a male teacher available. "School is for girls," he tells himself.*'

I find this dangerous stereotyping, which ignores some of the research into how schools, even at primary level, as shown in the Skelton research on male teachers and football, can promulgate the outdated 'boys will be boys' and 'boys are superior' philosophy. It ignores the fact that there are some noisy and badly behaved girls and some boys who are quite content with the quiet ethos of the learning environment. I don't recall either of my boys finding it difficult to cope with a well disciplined classroom or feeling that their skills in drawing, reading or writing were in any way inferior to the girls who were their peers. Personally I can't think of any more effective way of dividing the sexes and of making boys feel bad about themselves than by putting them into classes with girls who are a year older.

Biddulph's limited understanding of sexual politics and the history of the women's movement is, I think, revealed in a section of *Raising Boys* entitled 'Boys are not inferior, just different':

> '*Having a well developed left side of the brain, as boys tend to do, has many pluses. As well as having mathematical and mechanical abilities, males tend to be action oriented – if they see a problem they want to fix it. The right side of the brain handles both feelings and actions, so men are more likely to take action while women tend to mull over a problem to the point of total paralysis! It requires extra effort for a man to shift into his left hemisphere and find the words to explain the feelings he is registering in his right hemisphere.*

Germaine Greer has pointed out that there are more male geniuses in many fields, even though many may be unbalanced characters on the whole, needing someone to look after them (usually a woman!).

In an anti-male era, it's important to remember (and to show boys) that men built the planes, fought the wars, laid the railroad tracks, invented the cars, built the hospitals, invented the medicines and sailed the ships that made it all happen.'

Now I would question (and the evidence cited earlier in this chapter about opportunities for women clearly demonstrates it) that ours is an anti-male culture. Rather, it's a culture actually still struggling to give females and males real equality of opportunity and, contrary to popular perceptions, it's the males, not the females, who are still on the whole getting the better deal. Biddulph's is a wilful misreading of Germaine Greer's meaning about female genius. When she asserts that there have been fewer female than male geniuses she does not question women's ability to be brilliant (why should she, being quite brilliant herself!), merely their opportunities to show their brilliance, precisely because they were prevented from doing so by being responsible for the well-being of some damn man.

It would take me an unnecessary chunk of this chapter to knock down Biddulph's list of marvellous things that only men did by my citing contrasting examples of resourceful women who managed to battle through prevailing prejudice with the help of a handful of enlightened husbands and fathers who allowed them to develop and display their genius. Let's just mention two: Elizabeth Garret Anderson's Hospital for women and Marie Curie's contribution to medical science. I doubt we need to remind boys of how clever and powerful their gender traditionally has been seen to be – they get plenty of that in all aspects of their education – but we do need to teach them that women are to be equally admired and given the chance to make their contributions of genius to the advancement of humankind.

In *Schooling the Boys*, Christine Skelton questions the 'evolutionary biological' theory of the differences in the way male and

female brains function, in much the same way as I did in my introduction. I quoted research carried out by Professor Susan Greenfield.
Skelton draws on a substantial body of research to support her
contention that experience is far more likely to influence learning
patterns than any built in sex differences:

> 'Recent research into brain functioning has shown there is a
> tendency for males and females to use different parts of their brain
> for different higher order mental functions. Current thinking in
> neuroscience suggests that neuronal connections are selectively
> strengthened as a result of experience. Thus it can be argued that
> sex differences in brain function in such areas as mathematics and
> literacy are not innate, but are a result of being exposed to different
> experiences. This offers clear potential for development through
> ensuring that young babies and children are introduced to a wide
> range of experiences which will facilitate a broad range of learning
> styles.'

As parents we can do a lot to help our boys when they are very
small in those areas in which they are expected to be weak, and so
encourage those brain pathways to start working early on. Again I
can take none of the credit for the way my two developed their
dexterity in art, craft and writing. I'm a talker and voracious reader,
but have no artistic or practical talents at all. Not much patience
with small children either.

Jeanne our nanny was a genius at all things creative. The boys
were picking up scissors and cutting up coloured shapes from the
moment they were capable of holding something in their hands.
The kitchen was constantly awash with paints, paper, brushes and
water and I confess, frankly, to my frequent irritation at the mess.
So I sympathise with busy parents who don't have the luxury of full-
time childcare and have to do the creative stuff, cook the supper
and clear up themselves. But it is worth trying to spend time with
small boys in these kind of quiet, creative activities to better
prepare them for nursery and school.

The earliest framed painting of Ed's that I have was made when
he was about eighteen months old. It's just a load of brightly

coloured sploshes, but he had learned to hold a paintbrush and manipulate a tool from being very tiny, and he loving every minute.

I came into my own with talking and reading. I chattered away from the moment they were born and, most importantly, listened, even in those early weeks and months when nothing but babble comes back at you. But if they made sounds, I copied them and we engaged in conversation right from the start, instinctively. I read to them from birth too and they both loved listening to stories and looking at books. Jeanne, a frustrated teacher if ever there was one, would play 'look say' with them in their high chair as a game. She made up cards with letters and pictures, progressing to words as soon as they could sit up independently and they seemed to love deciphering the codes. Both were fluent speakers and readers by the time they went to nursery at three and enjoyed books, both reading for themselves and being read to, up to about the age of twelve.

Then something went wrong with Ed. He suffered from what so many boys suddenly get infected with – a loss of interest in reading. First of all he'd joke that he couldn't see the point in reading for himself when he had a professional with a famous voice to do it for him (me). When I insisted he should read for himself he just stopped. The only time he was jolted out of his literary torpor was when the school insisted the boys write an essay on their wider reading. He spent a Christmas holiday galloping through Melvyn Burgess' *Junk* and Jane Austen's *Pride and Prejudice*, wrote the essay, and then gave up again. Ed prides himself on the fact that the only 'B' he got in his GCSEs was in English Literature, for which he'd never read any of the set texts, just the cribs.

So, there was nothing wrong with his ability to read and he didn't fit any of the popular theories, which seek to explain why boys don't read. He was wired up as well as any girl from experience as a baby and there was no lack of interest in narrative or stories about relationships – he's long been a fan of programmes like *Hollyoaks* and *East Enders*. I think he gave up reading because of cultural pressure. Partly from me – so it was a minor rebellion to refuse to do something I thought was so important – and partly from the culture around him. Boy+book = swot/girlie. My gender too may well have fed into this equation. I'm demonstrably the big reader in the family and, of course, I'm a girl!

In Ed's case I didn't worry. I knew he was perfectly literate and would cope with his exams and the reading of textbooks without any trouble. He really didn't need to excel in literature, as his plan was to concentrate on science and I suspected, as has been the case, that he would come to reading later in life. He's now reading books about his business which interest him and he still gets his need for narrative satisfied by TV, films and the theatre. I only feel sad for him that he doesn't get the pleasure I derive from sitting down and burying himself in a good read.

Charlie, too, was infected to a lesser degree by the 'uncool' image of reading fiction, although, as he leans more towards the arts side – English, philosophy and languages – he's becoming more interested in reading again and was actually caught on a train the other day buried in *The Lord of the Flies*.

If your boys go through a period of not being avid readers of literature I would advise being relaxed about it, as long as you know their reading up to early teenage has not been a problem. If you really are anxious you could try taking the TV out of their room and encouraging their father or any other males around to be seen reading fiction (fathers who've done a lot of reading to their sons are said to be a great help in reducing the girlie image of reading, although I've found no research to support this).

Other parents' experiences have been a little more positive than mine. Diane Abbott, like a number of the parents I spoke to, said J. K. Rowling deserves every penny she has earned from *Harry Potter*.

'I've always read to my son – but it hasn't been easy being a single parent who works eighteen hours a day, but I always made time to read to him at night. There's no TV in his room and I insist he goes up to bed at eight. He's the only child in his circle who didn't see Big Brother. *James is eleven now, and there was a short blip when he didn't read, he would just listen to music when he was in his room and then along came* Harry Potter *and he loved it. Now he goes up to his bedroom without complaint and reads for himself.'*

Jenny Stephen had no problems with any of her boys. You'll remember she'd cleared the lower shelves for their books for easy access and she and Martin are both passionately interested in books and reading themselves.

> 'Going to bookshops and buying books was a treat the whole family enjoyed together for as long as I can remember. We both read to them all the time and when Neil, the eldest started to be an independent reader, he would come home from school, tidy his room and sit down to read. The others rather followed his example. The routine for relaxation became curling up with a book.'

From a professional point of view, the Stephens both agree that it's something of a myth that boys don't read, although they acknowledge that they both teach in schools where boys are clever and well motivated. In Jenny's view, neither boys nor girls do enough reading, as there are far too many other distractions in the form of TVs, computers and game consoles, reinforcing the argument that none of these entertainments should be in a child's room. (Advice I singularly failed to follow.)

The over-emphasis on differences between genders can mask the important question of differences within genders. Clare Wigzell's experience illustrates the question perfectly. Her three boys share the same genetic background and enjoyed the same type of schooling, the same parental involvement, the same level of reading to them and with them and the same amount of support at home. Two are successful academically – George is predicated two 'A's and a 'B' at A level and has had offers from every university where he's applied to study drama. He has a solid circle of dependable friends, is happy and trouble free.

Elliott, on the other hand, the middle son, doesn't read, prefers his skateboard and graffiti art to his homework and likes to be out with a set of streetwise friends who are always on the verge of trouble. Clare considered moving him to a different school, but the only possible option was too far for him to travel. Boarding school was not an option, as Clare was not prepared to risk him feeling he had been cut adrift. Clare sees her job as protecting and supporting

Elliott in the things he is good at – particularly his art – and keeping open lines of communication, bearing in mind all the time that he is, at heart, a great kid.

> *'I've always encouraged my boys to be emotional and confident – possibly one of the reasons he has such a reputation for being cheeky – he'll always stand up for himself. He was bullied by a group of Asian boys recently and he handled himself brilliantly. Being streetwise can come in very handy. Most importantly, though, he was helping out with some very young children not very long ago and we found this tough, difficult middle boy of ours was marvellous with young children, quite exceptional. He had so much patience and would show them what they wanted over and over and over again. It's these things we have to look for and build on and the school should be doing the same. Our experience reinforces my belief that when you talk about difference it's not a boy/girl thing, it's to do with being different people.'*

Where there is a real problem with boys' literacy, as there seems to be with Elliott, there is some research which suggests we should, as Clare suggests, begin to ease the literary emphasis in the school and the national curriculum and place value on the things they choose to read in order to help boys like him. In *What About the Boys*, Christine Hall and Martin Coles, researchers in literacy at the University of Nottingham say that,

> *'Our findings show clearly that popular anxiety about an overall decline in the amount of children's book reading is unfounded. Most children read regularly outside school, but there is a tendency towards fewer books being read by children, as they grow older. Newspaper and magazine reading has increased among children. What the figures also show, of course, is that boys read slightly less than girls – and that they have been reading less than girls for twenty-five years. Nor was this a new phenomenon in the 1970s. A survey conducted by Jenkinson in 1940 indicated the same pattern . . . But the real problem now is not about about the relative performance of boys on the one hand and girls on the other, but of some boys and some girls.'*

Hall and Coles' findings show that both boys and girls enjoy reading fiction, and have proved it a myth that boys enjoy reading only non-fiction. Only 2 per cent of all children in their survey chose non-fiction as their exclusive reading diet. But the researchers did find that both boys and girls read a lot of comics, magazines, periodicals, newspapers and fanzines (whether of football or pop stars). This led to another important finding – that boys' magazine reading tends to lead them to socialise with each other by analysing information, swapping facts and figures, scores and club histories; whereas girls' magazines and the social relations they cement as a result tend to be about relationships and life stories. (A good argument, in my view, for publishers to find that 'holy grail' – the magazine for younger teenage boys that has more in it than football.)

Thus girls' vernacular reading equips them well for the kind of literature they will be expected to cope with at school; boys' vernacular reading does not adapt them so well and may be another reason why some of them reject 'girlie' books and see reading as a 'feminine' activity. With this in mind, the researchers advocate broadening the reading opportunities children have in school, particularly to benefit those who are reluctant or unable to tackle the books on the curriculum.

> 'We need readers who can be attentive to and skilled in reading associative patterns and making links. Screen reading brings with it none of the features of closure and the sense of an ending which are the classic elements of the study of fiction – the links and associations can go on indefinitely, layered one upon the other. And, in some respects, this important aspect of computer screen literacy is related to reading texts on film or television screens. It is clear that the amorphous metaphor of the web is fundamentally different from the patterning of book-based literary forms. Literacy teaching about elements such as style, diction, form, audience and purpose would need to be approached differently if it was really our intention to value and develop screen reading in school.
>
> This is not to argue that teaching pupils to appreciate literature

is unimportant. On the contrary, we regard the teaching of fiction as fundamental to the development of literacy and to establishing a sense of cultural continuity. But we need to broaden the focus of the school literacy curriculum beyond its current emphasis upon the literary and the narrative, with its tentative nods in the direction of non-fiction, media and computer literacies.'

So, no need to get unduly worried about the computer, the *Beano* or a tabloid newspaper!

Choosing a school for our boys can be fraught with difficulties. Like Clare, Jackie Kay had similar problems with her son finding 'suitable' friends in his first secondary school, so she decided to move him.

'He did have a bunch of friends at his old school that were a bad influence on him, so I moved his school. Now all of that is much better. Oddly enough, I'd sent him to a school where there were lots of other black kids, but then he got into this whole black boy cool image thing and started behaving like somebody I didn't recognise. It was very strange for me to try and work out, but moving to a different school has made a difference. He likes books and basket-ball and dogs a lot. At the moment he's thinking of being a dog psychologist! I don't know how I'd cope with that! Rap is the thing I find most difficult because the lyrics are so misogynist and to have this teenage boy memorising the 'mother fucking' lines is quite distressing. So that is now the biggest challenge. I think I am managing to get him to broaden his musical taste.'

This is a big problem for Diane Abbott who's just at the stage where she is trying to decide what to do for James as he turns the corner into secondary school. Her difficulties are exacerbated by the fact that she is the MP for Hackney and needs to send him to a school close to her home in the constituency. She's also a Labour MP so whatever decision she makes for her child will be politically sensitive.

'Already I've found he has to be one of the boys in primary school and he's becoming dismissive of school, work, books. He has to be one of the posse and was terrified I would make him do violin

because of the harm it would do to his street cred. I backed off that one. At home he reads and has an extensive vocabulary, although you wouldn't know that if you heard him talking to his friends. I heard him say recently, "That Cheryl, I called her a Medusa head". I was horrified.

I constantly have to drill into him there's no point copying the ways of others. He will be the first to get into trouble because he's a boy and he's black. I've told him he must sit still and pay attention in class. I'm very insistent about his classroom behaviour. Otherwise he'll find it too seductive to be one of the boys.

He goes to secondary school this September so I went to see his teacher to see how he's doing. He's in the top set, so he's doing OK. I asked who else was in the top set and they were all girls. It's a real problem in these inner city schools, the lad culture is so strong, it's the girls who're doing well and if a boy does work hard and is bright he ends up with the girls. It's hard.

And now the question of secondary school. Secondary education in Hackney is in a state of collapse. Some of these inner city schools I wouldn't send my worst enemies' sons to. There's a male youth culture there I dread. I've watched friends struggling with this issue. They've sent their sons to the local comprehensive school and watched them get sucked into a social persona where they hide under a hoodie and listen to rap and once a boy is absorbed by it, it's hard to get him out.

Boys benefit from structure and boundaries and they just don't get it. In lessons they're spaced out on drugs and the teachers don't challenge them, they just turn a blind eye. The average GCSE results are five A to E grades, which is dreadful. There's a drug culture and a knife culture and a friend's son was shot in the chest with an air rifle. I don't want that. I'm so frustrated because there's no middle way. It's either fee paying or these terrible schools. We tried for one of the Guild schools and he dropped one point on his verbal reasoning so he didn't get in.

We now have a situation which is the worst form of the 11 Plus. I went to a state grammar school and did very well there. Now the ratio of places at these good schools is much smaller than when I was that age. There are hundreds of concerned parents trying to get them in. Dozens of these poor kids turn up for tests at several schools and so many of them are disappointed. It's awful and I really don't know what I'm going to do.

I know that the most important determining factor in how well a child, whether it's a boy or a girl, does at school is the family background. All my family are very bright and we can deal with helping him with the academic side of things, but it's this male youth culture that's being allowed to run riot that I dread.'

Lynne Segal has few regrets about the way she raised her son, apart from his education. She would certainly sympathise with the agonies of choice Diane is now grappling with.

'Those mothers like me who sent their children to inner city comprehensives in the '70s and '80s all found our children were simply not being given any sort of adequate education to prepare them for higher education or the professions. The milieu of the school thus proved downwardly mobile for them. They were teased, not only by peers, but even teachers, if they didn't fit the basically anti-swot school mode.

This has been immensely distressing for all of us and we did not then feel able to do anything about it, though we did complain to teachers. It's a permanent source of bitterness, solved now, of course, by almost all of my friends in inner London by sending their children to private school.

I hate this with all my heart and soul that, so early, we are shoring up the existing class system so definitively. It's anathema. But my son, like almost all his other friends (often girls as well as boys) who were children of parents like me found it very hard "choosing a career", something they were simply not educated to do.

Most now have jobs in computing or the lower echelons of the media world, though it took my son and all his friends from Islington Green School (which we learned long after was one of the worst in London, although hyped at the time as progressive and certainly very anti sexist/racist) quite a while to settle into any jobs. But many, like my son, feel that somehow they are a disappointment to their parents.

I do not see this as intrinsically a problem to do with sons, except that there is probably even more pressure on them to feel "successful" when they don't. I see this, above all, as the near total failure of our educational policy. I often discuss this with my fellow feminist mothers these days. It makes us weep.

He is not at all competitive, indeed not competitive enough for this world. I feel I failed him in terms of preparing him for the world as it is today (not to mention sending him to one of the worst comprehensives in the country) where both men and women are far more individualistic, competitive and goal seeking than he was raised to be.'

Diane Abbott, as someone who wields influence in political circles, might take a look at a book, *Ahead of the Class*, written recently by Lady Marie Stubbs who at the age of sixty and only six weeks after her retirement was asked to take over the failing St George's School in London's Maida Vale. It became infamous when its head teacher, Philip Lawrence, was assaulted and killed at the school gates and since that time had slipped into a parlous state. The school had a reputation for violence amongst pupils and there were attacks on staff. Lady Stubbs describes it as, 'The school itself is a dull, lifeless museum with an air of exhaustion and despair. It feels like an out of control youth club, with some lessons now and then.'

By sheer force of personality and with a small team of like-minded staff around her Lady Stubbs transformed the school within a year. She brightened up the decorations and put notices up all over the school offering guidance as to expected behaviour. 'Walk Don't Run' and 'Single File', for instance. She put interesting posters and pictures on the walls and called herself headmistress, rather than head teacher.

Stubbs introduced herself personally to every pupil and intervened to stop fights physically, placing herself at risk of danger, as she never knew at the beginning of her time there whether the boys might be carrying knives or not. She managed to persuade parents to come to the school, and chewed gum and wore a baseball cap whilst talking to them to demonstrate how inappropriate it was for their children to appear that way at school. She introduced more structured teaching, insisted pupils turn up on time and replaced the tired staff who weren't happy with her methods with others who were energetic and enthusiastic.

She sums up her philosophy as 'old-fashioned values combined with respect for each and every child – an emphasis on politeness, discipline, boundaries and common sense. Also an interest in the children – I don't call them kids, it's disrespectful – a desire to make them all feel worthwhile and included'. Lady Stubbs achieved what she had been asked to do – removing the school from special measures – and improved matters equally for boys and girls within a year. There are hints that the new Education Secretary, Charles Clarke, may be open to this kind of disciplined approach to comprehensive schooling. He is said to be keen to replace heads who 'can't hack it', but there seems, still, to be a long way to go.

Diane Abbott does seem to be right that constant and powerful intervention at home can be a determining factor in whether a bright child does well at school or not. A recent survey by Stephen Ball, Professor of Sociology at the University of London, showed that an involved and interested parent (he balks at 'pushy mum', although his work shows that it is still mothers who are primarily concerned with their children's education) is the secret of school success. 'She ensures her child is seen as clever by paying for extra coaching and making sure her offspring moves "in the right circles" even if she doesn't pay for private education.'

Jackie Kay is convinced that boys don't motivate themselves as easily as girls – although I suspect this has more to do with this business of being seen as an uncool swot than with intrinsic gender differences. It's hard, it seems, to be one of the guys if you've done your homework. Jackie says, 'I'm always having to push him and I'd really much preferred it if he pushed himself.'

I'm afraid I made the choice of sending my boys to a single sex, fee paying, northern grammar school in Manchester, partly, as I've already explained, because of its attempts to address the gender questions which concerned me, but also because it demands high academic standards and is highly disciplined. It certainly worked in Ed's case. Charlie does his GCSE's next year, so it's too soon to tell, but I rarely have to push him to get on with his homework, as a fate worse than death awaits him at school if he lags behind.

I didn't want to pay for private education, as, like Lynne Segal, I believe profoundly that in an ideal world all children should have equal chances. But, like so many others, I couldn't sacrifice my boys' future to my political instincts. It would not have been my choice to send them to an all boys' school, as I believe the only way to encourage boys and girls to get to know and respect each other is to educate them together in schools that pay close attention to helping them understand gender relations, but, as so few schools seemed to have the faintest clue about how to do it, I chose to go down a more traditional route and, academically, it seems to be paying off.

I absolutely abhor the cliché that so many parents trot out. 'If I had a girl I'd send her to an all girls' school because she'll fare better academically, a boy I'll send to a mixed school because the girls will civilize him.' It is profoundly irritating when all boys are portrayed as uncontrollable monsters and girls as the goody goodies who'll calm them down. Neither, as we've seen, is the case.

In the rush to try and address the (I believe exaggerated) gap between girls and boys, some co-educational schools are experimenting with single sex classes in those subjects in which the boys appear not to do as well as girls, notably English and foreign languages. One teacher at King's School, a mixed comprehensive for eleven to sixteen year olds in Winchester, where this kind of experiment has been conducted, describes the difference between boys and girls in her school thus, 'Give most girls a map to copy and they'll do it. Boys will question the point of the exercise and volunteer to go to the photocopier.'

One of the boys in her French class said, 'I have more fun in my mixed lessons, but I learn more when I'm with the lads. In mixed classes, girls get all the attention by being brainy, so I get it back by being bad.'

The school's head of English, Rob Jekyll, responsible for boys' achievement says:

'We adapt the system for the needs of boys in the same way as we would adapt it for pupils with a specific learning difficulty. The girls also benefit because potentially troublesome boys are removed from

their classes. The boys' class is not dependent on having a male teacher – women teachers are often better with them. But you do need someone in charge who is firm, methodical and quick witted.'

The school proudly announced that in 1998, 69 per cent of boys gained at least five GCSEs at grades A* to C compared with 73 per cent of girls. This year, the boys at King's overtook the girls: 82 per cent gained five top grades, compared with 79 per cent of girls. I worry slightly at a school seeming to crow that things are now sort of as they should be with boys in their proper place, ahead of the game!

In March 2003 Winchester was included in a study of four schools involved in similar programmes carried out by academics at Homerton College in Cambridge. The pilot study concluded that using single sex groups was a significant factor in establishing a school culture that would raise educational standards.

At Comberton Village College in Cambridgeshire, one of the other schools in the study, fourteen year olds have been taught in single sex English classes for five years to try to narrow a 20 per cent gap between boys and girls in GCSE. Last year the gap was said to fall to 5 per cent. Mary Martin, the head teacher said,

'It became apparent very quickly that single sex groups made for a more settled climate and classes that were more conducive to working. The girls studied novels such as Jane Austen's Pride and Prejudice, *while the boys read works that would appeal to them more, such as* Touching the Void *by Joe Simpson, a first-person account of mountain survival.'*

(Note, the research has not revealed, because it hasn't asked, how well or otherwise the girls are doing compared with the boys in the more traditionally 'male' subjects, such as maths and science.) Given that the other academics quoted at the beginning of this chapter question whether there is much of a gender gap in education at all, and presented with the kind of stereotyping that leaps out of the traditional choice of reading just quoted (pity the poor boys who might love Lizzie Bennett and Mr Darcy and the girls who might long to be exposed to tales of adventure and derring do), it would be disappointing if the government, as it's suggested it might, is tempted to leap into this form of gender segregation to sort out a problem that many are convinced does not really exist.

In choosing a school for your child, you have to make up your own mind, as I did, what best suits him from what's currently available. But segregation seems to me to be a sticking plaster over a much more serious and damaging wound. Are we really to accept that boys and girls, men and women, can only be effective when they are separated or are there ways of creating an environment where both sexes can be hardworking, sensible, educated beyond stereotype and satisfied with what's on offer and the way it's taught?

We should also be looking, in my view, as I suggested with regard to sex education, at the question of properly formulated and informed gender education. Christine Skelton in *Schooling the Boys* pleads for an end, as early as primary education, to 'referring to projects for boys and talk instead of gender equity programmes'.

> 'The strategy of down-playing if not eradicating gender differences seems to have been one of the aims of equal opportunities policies in the '80s. This is not to say that equal opportunities policies were unhelpful as they did a great deal in raising awareness of the ways in which pupils were routinely organised and managed along gender lines; the traditional stereotypes to be found in reading schemes and other school resources; and the predominance of men as head teachers and working exclusively with older pupils. What children cannot be fooled into thinking is that gender does not matter, nor can they be persuaded that it is acceptable, even desirable – to traverse gender boundaries. An alternative and more appropriate agenda is to put into place initiatives that encourage children to think about their own position – to get them to question some of the more taken-for-granted aspects of what they see, hear, read, think, act out.'

Skelton tells a very simple story which illustrates how easily this can be done. She was talking to a group of six-year-old girls at Bentwood school and one of the girls kept asking Christine if she had 'any bairns'. She asked several times, even though Christine kept answering 'No'.

'When I replied "No" again her look of curiosity was replaced by one of complete incomprehension and she asked in a baffled tone, "How?" I was the first adult woman she had come across who did not have children. Disrupting children's own conventional images of masculinity and feminity does not necessarily always mean introducing radical alternatives – sometimes it simply means telling them how it is.'

In *What About the Boys* Michael C Reichert points to the possible dangers of paying attention to boys without asking them to 'rethink masculinity'.

'Lavish attention has not historically produced boys who are better off. Lefkovitz's 1997 chronicle of the most popular and darling boys in a New Jersey town's High School, who mistook the town's indulgence towards them as permission to abuse and rape, reminds us that attention alone does not necessarily free boys for healthier or more just lives.'

Reichert was the psychologist involved in developing gender awareness programmes at the Haverford School – a boys' senior day school in South Eastern Pennsylvania. They worked with girls from a couple of neighbouring schools with the aim of giving boys and girls a chance to inform each other about the experience of being male or female. The first programme consisted of six hours of discussions and exercises to look at the role gender plays in dating, sex, friendships, families and education.

'Boys came fearful of "male bashing" while girls came expecting to have to fight for a voice. Largely student driven, the workshops evolved to include dialogues, skits, exercises, talks by male and female facilitators and opportunities for the boys and girls to listen closely to each other. In the closing circle of the first workshop both boys and girls expressed the satisfaction that they had joined hands to resist gender's limitations. One powerful outcome for the workshop was an organised effort by boys to challenge sexist comments and assumptions at their school more vigorously.'

It is becoming obvious that boys are hungry for this kind of education, because they too are aware of the bad reputation they have in schools and want to do something about it. Professor Stephen Frosh from Birkbeck College at the University of London, together with Dr Ann Phoenix and Dr Rob Pattman of the Open University published the results of a survey they conducted among fourteen-year-old boys in *The Psychologist* in February 2003. The boys came from a range of twelve secondary schools in London, including private and state, single sex and co-educational. They were interviewed in groups and individually.

The researchers found that, contrary to common belief, boys were eager to think and talk about their lives and the apparent contradictions in their behaviour. It become apparent that the boys were confused and muddled by the popular perception that conscientiousness and commitment to work are seen as feminine traits, while unruly behaviour is thought to be masculine. In individual interviews the boys said they admired the girls for working hard and were critical of boys for being obsessive about football and having a relative lack of interest in their schoolwork.

Appearing masculine when talking in a group was considered important and boys who did not display typical male behaviour were accused of being effeminate or gay. But in individual interviews many of them recognised the injustices of racism and homophobia and said they were aware that social class is divisive. The researchers concluded.

'Our research brought home to us how rich and full of expression can be the accounts boys give of their lives. The image of the angrily grunting and inarticulate teenager is not one that stands up to scrutiny when boys are given the opportunity to reflect on their experiences and are encouraged to talk. They talked about uncertainties over friendships, anger with absent or unavailable fathers, feelings of rejection and "stuckness" in relationships, ideas about girls and fears and aspirations for the future. Given the opportunity, many young, teenage boys are eager to think and talk about their lives and about how to make things better.'

CHAPTER SEVEN

DADS AND LADS

'The majority now absolutely believes that women can do what men can do, but the next step is to believe that men can do what women can do' (Gloria Steinem)

In the previous chapter it became apparent that it's not enough to say boys need male role models to help them fit comfortably into a new world of gender relations. In the discussion about male teachers the vital question was, 'What kind of male role models do we want boys to have?' Christine Skelton in *Schooling the Boys* makes the point that fathers have an enormous influence as role models, too, but their effect on their sons is not necessarily benign. In one of the primary schools she studied there was a high percentage of the oft-criticised single mother, yet,

'The two most alienated, disruptive and violent boys were from notorious local families whose involvement in crime was managed by a hierarchy of fathers, uncles and cousins. These two boys had a surfeit of male role models.'

If Dads want to be helpful to their lads they too have to struggle with conventional views of what it means to be masculine and ask themselves what kind of example they are setting if they work excessively long hours, fail to take equal responsibility for the running of the household and worrying about childcare and drag their boys to football regardless of whether they want to be there or not.

No one pretends this is an easy balance to achieve. We live in a society where work outside the home is much more highly valued than what goes on inside the home, where a family's status often depends on the amount of material wealth it demonstrates in the possessions it owns and where traditional ideas about masculinity, power and winning the bread are deeply entrenched. There is still enormous pressure on young males to do well in their education, get a good job, earn a lot of money and support a family, but we've gone beyond the point where any refusal on the part of men and boys to engage in new thinking about domestic responsibilities and family life is sustainable.

It is worth mentioning at this stage, especially if you are wondering how on earth you would manage financially if one of you gave up work or you both went part-time, that a survey carried out in March 2003 by the *Big Toe Radio Show*, BBC7's children's programme, found that 77 per cent of children said they would prefer their parents to earn less money and spend more time with their family, even it meant that holidays were less fancy and there was no money for the trendiest trainers. Funny how no one seems to have thought of asking the children before.

Women and girls, as I've indicated earlier, have been voting with their feet in protest at the impossible burdens of double shifting. Some of them are being forced again to make the choice that women used to make before we gave girls the idea that they could 'have it all'. They would like to have a husband, a family and a career, but realise it's probably not going to be possible, so they turn their backs on the prospect of a family life altogether.

I know too many others, highly educated, immersed in jobs they love and successfully climbing the career ladder who fall in love, have children and hit, to their shock and often deep resentment, the Allerednic syndrome. Some happily make the choice to stay at home or work part-time, others are forced into it and their relationships founder, frequently leaving two bitter parents and children miserably bouncing back and forth.

Boys are beginning to be aware of this dilemma and the kind of readjustments to the way families are expected to work that they may have to make. Some are the victims of broken or miserable relationships themselves and have no wish to repeat the patterns their parents struggled through; most have been raised alongside a generation of girls for whom equality of opportunity is a given, but for whom we, the older generations, have done relatively little to give a better template for a successful new kind of family life. The bottom line, whether you're male or female, is that you really can't 'have it all', but it should never be assumed it's the woman or the man who will stay at home and look after the family.

'Horses for courses' is the best way to regard it. In my case, as I've already said, after struggling with nannies who would never match up to Jeanne, it was David's suggestion that he stay home and be the full-time parent. He had left the Navy, had not really found another compelling career path, felt the boys would benefit from having one of us taking care of them and had no qualms about deciding it should be him. He was right. I would have been very unhappy to give up a job I loved, and have never been adept at occupying small children. He's had a great time, thoroughly enjoying the company of his sons. He's endured the demands of the domestic work and hasn't always achieved the standards demanded by this Yorkshire matriarch, but hey, immaculate homes are pretty sterile places. (She repeats through gritted teeth whilst wiping the kitchen surfaces down yet again. Please tell me an inability to see crumbs and grease is not genetic, but studied incompetence on his part which ensures I carry out a small share of the housework!)

Now, as the boys are growing away and David's in his late forties, like most women who have taken a long break, he's finding his way back into the outside world. He has no ambition to go back into electronic engineering and join the rat race at fifty. Instead he's doing voluntary work for a community radio station and hoping it will eventually lead to paid employment. He is, though, still regarded in some quarters as rather strange and gets very cross when anyone calls him Mr Murray!

Jenny Stephen holds discussions about these issues in her school and told me about one sixth-form boy's particularly poignant cry. He was, she says, unsure about his role. On some occasions, he explained, he was expected to be chivalrous and act like an old-fashioned man, opening doors and getting up to give his seat to a woman; in other places, those kind of things didn't seem to matter or were considered laughably outdated. He was aware he would be required to know how to cook supper and at some point would have to consider the impact of having babies and who would look after them. He would also be expected to be a wage earner, but felt that, if he did need to have time off from work to look after his children, as a father he would get less under-standing at work than as a mother.

The positive involvement of dads in helping their boys through this minefield is essential, so it's certainly not helpful when research by the Equal Opportunities Commission – trumpeting the fact that today's fathers of under fives are now spending two hours on a weekday and around six and a half hours on a weekend with their children, compared with the fifteen minutes their forbears spent a generation ago – is greeted with the kind of retrograde rubbish written by Matt Seaton in an article in *The Guardian*. I quote it more or less in full as a reminder, to those of us who want to see more equity in family relationships, of what we up against.

'According to the EOC report, the new model touchy feely father would be at home even more if only he were less worried that he would be seen as a work-shy wimp by his bosses and colleagues for claiming flexible hours and trotting off early to spend some extra time with his kids.

Ah, that "if only". "If only", says the father to the EOC researcher, summoning a misty look in his eye and a plaintive note to his voice. "Of course, I'd like nothing more than to spend more time at home with my little darlings, but look at me – I'm completely a prisoner of the macho long hours' culture of this place." Boxes ticked, the researcher moves on to the next interview; father gets back to the pressing priorities of his working life – visiting eBay to check the status of his bid on the portable beer cooler . . .

Combined with the "Quick drink after work" with a colleague (note to partner, if you're reading this, that was actually the impor-tant marketing meeting I told you about), this father's unflagging commitment to putting in time at the office ensured that he sadly spent rather less than two hours with his children. To be precise eleven minutes; of which seven were spent ignoring them, three yelling at them to stop shouting at each other and one explaining that he really wasn't qualified to give an opinion on who is the best fighter in Dragon Ball Z and that, frankly, he couldn't give a monkeys.

Of course, we all aspire to be better parents, even fathers. We would all like to give our children more of our time. But where the EOC research is seriously flawed, I believe, is that it does not take into account what I call the theoretical physics of parenthood. Anyone who has spent time with small children will have experienced quantum mechanics as applied to childcare: according to an unpublished theorem of Albert Einstein – a notable absentee father: he knew something that guy (author's note to Steve Biddulph – how many potential female Einstein's were just left holding the baby?) – the closer you approach a young child, and the younger the child, the more time itself becomes "sticky", as physicists say, and slows down. This is why, for example, it often seems to take hours to get a baby to sleep, and then their naps appear to last for only a few seconds (known as the barely-time-to-make-a-coffee effect).

The converse also holds true: put some distance between you and the child and time speeds up again. The father we spoke to, for instance, was astounded when told that he had spent more than twelve hours absent from the family home; to him, the time had passed in a blur that amounted to just a few minutes of "subjective time".

The paradox of this phenomenon is that it seems to apply mainly to men. Women rarely report the sensation, whereas men regularly notice that the minutes spent supervising their toddlers' activities or helping with their kids' homework or playing family board games stretch out as they have not done since they themselves were school kids in the first period of a double maths lesson. Some difference in brain chemistry is suspected that renders men more susceptible to finding the company of small children crushingly dull.

The truth of the matter, of course, is that we men are work-shy *wimps. That's why we prefer to stay in the office, in the safe and undemanding refuge of the long-hours culture and our bread-winning role. Believe me, we know where the real work goes on – which is why we're shy of it.'*

Remember what I said about the quality of the male role model. Matt Seaton, mildly amusing though his turn of phrase may be, isn't it. It really does make you wonder why men like him bother to have children at all. (Which is what would be said about any woman who dared confess that her young children are boring and that she preferred to be at work than at home looking after them. Seaton might be surprised to find a lot of them do suffer from sticky time syndrome, it's just not considered acceptable for them to say so.) It certainly makes me wonder how long Mrs Seaton will be prepared to service his idling at the office whilst she endures 'the crushingly dull company' of his small children.

There are, though, many more hopeful signs of positive change than Seaton would have us believe. Jack O'Sullivan who, only a few years ago was an Associate Editor at the *Independent* and was offered a senior editorial job at another newspaper, decided to turn down the offer. He opted instead to be a more involved father for his children – he has a daughter of six and a son of a year – and to start his own pressure group Fathers Direct. (Not to be confused with Families Need Fathers – an organisation whose reputation was damaged in the late '70s and early '80s when it was alleged that separated fathers were encouraged by the organisation to adopt a confrontational manner with mothers over access rights and, in some cases, were advised to abduct their children if there were difficulties.) Running the group Fathers Direct, publishing its newsletter *Father Work* and writing as a freelance journalist could be done primarily from home, giving O'Sullivan a chance to balance his work and family life.

He began to bring the issue of fathers' involvement at home into the public arena long before sporting heroes such as David Beckham and Michael Owen made a baby as much of a designer accessory for a young man as a Moschino t-shirt and a pair of Versace pants. Jack does, though, acknowledge their importance as models for young fathers and quotes Jude, a nineteen-year-old lad from South London with no job, no home of his own and no money who became full-time Dad to his son, Rushaun, when the baby was three months old and his mother was no longer around. Jude still has no job – he looks after the boy full-time – and the two of them live in a sparsely furnished council flat.

Jude described himself to Jack as the eldest in a family of seven.

'I'm used to caring for my brothers and sisters. I'm young, so Rushaun learns more from me and it's easier to be a role model. I have my youth and energy. I have time to do what Rushaun enjoys. I can see life growing in him, every little advancement. It's taken me two years to get the feel for being a father. I've had to look around and take it all in. At first I felt like an alien. I'm the oldest of seven so my mum has six others to cope with and can't do that much for us. I have to do it for myself.'

O'Sullivan has nothing but praise for celebrity role models such as Beckham because they help young fathers like Jude feel less of an alien. 'Beckham,' he writes, 'of course, has no problem with the breadwinner bit, but his distinguishing characteristic is his public endorsement of caring fatherhood. For a young dad, perhaps with little else to offer, this can be a liberation.'

Jack also quotes Celestine Agbo, who has worked with young dads for more than twenty years and described how he established a young fathers' group during the World Cup.

'I put an advert in the paper for meetings of a David Beckham Supporters Club. I got a few phone calls. It turned out that six – nearly half the people who rang – were young men with children. Once I asked them about their kids, they got really excited discussing them. I think it is because, often, when young dads get into relationships, no-one wants to talk to them about their kids, so it's refreshing for them.'

O'Sullivan and Fathers Direct are creative – as you would expect from a professional journalist – in getting their concerns and their activities covered in the national press. He still produces what Jack describes as their 'trade' glossy, *Father Work*. It's designed to inform professionals about how they can help fathers get more positively involved with their children and it teems with inspiring role models. Jack mentioned to me a school in the Rhonda Valley where a far-sighted headmaster recognised that fathers were the great, untapped educational resource in the region of his primary school and sent some off to be trained by Fathers Direct. They're now making a good contribution to the school and their children's education.

It's widely recognised that a father who reads to his boys and is seen to be a reader himself will help alleviate some of the difficulties some boys have with seeing reading as a purely female pursuit. Indeed, recent research carried out by Charles Lewis, Professor of developmental psychology at the University of Lancaster has shown that good paternal involvement – or lack of it – can decisively influence children's outcomes in life, such as academic success and criminality.

Oxford University's Centre for Research into Parenting and Children agrees independently with Lewis's results, highlights the importance of the good-father-son relationship on the boy's healthy emotional and academic development, finding that such boys are less likely to suffer from behavioural difficulties as teenagers, or brushes with the police later in life. The researchers class an involved father as one who reads to his child, takes outings with him and is interested in his education.

The study showed that age seven is the most important time during which a father can influence his child's later educational achievement, even earlier is preferable, as a father who starts early, is likely to continue throughout the child's life. The researchers, also, in their definition of father, include a biological father who doesn't live with the child's mother or someone who isn't the natural father, but is a good stepfather, grandfather or family friend. A broken home, they say, does not necessarily diminish the father-figure factor, but the father has to do something other than just be there, hiding behind the newspaper with his pipe and slippers.

Nevertheless, whilst many fathers say they would like to be involved – recent research by the Department of Education shows that, while three-quarters of fathers were willing, only 12 per cent claimed to be more involved than their partner in their boys' education, compared with 72 per cent of women.

Fathers also said they didn't know how to contribute. A government initiative (in my view – given my reservations about sporty stereotyping – rather unfortunately entitled A *Winning Team*, based on a footballing theme), made some suggestions. It recommends that fathers take their boys shopping, and work out prices with them, as they go around the shop, and the cost of the bill at the check out to help with maths and general knowledge about the way the world works. The researchers thought it a good idea for dads to watch quiz programmes with their lads to hone their wider knowledge, to show that they were interested in 'knowing stuff' and to discuss magazines, books and newspapers with them.

The initiative also strongly advised that fathers, like mothers, make the time and effort to attend parents' evenings at school. It seems to me vital that fathers take an interest in these matters. It's so obviously hopeless for boys, particularly those of eleven to fourteen who are looking to their fathers for clues as to how to be a man, if Dad seems to be too distant to be interested in what they are learning, how they are behaving, who their friends are and how their thinking is developing. Education and social relations must not be seen to be female preserves.

I would, by the way, take issue with some newly published research by Professor Charles Lewis, which suggests play-fights with Daddy makes boys grow up happier. He says, 'There is something special about rough-house play with dads, and that helps a child to learn self-control.' My poor David has been missing his front teeth since one of these incidents when Charlie was about two. They were rolling around on the floor, tickling, cuffing and squealing when Charlie decided to head butt his Dad in the mouth. Unfortunately two-year-olds do not have self-control and a father's teeth are too big a price to pay. The study does say that children whose fathers are physical with them are amongst the friendliest, most easy-going and popular at school. It may be wiser to read physical as cuddly and physically affectionate. In play fighting, as in real fighting, people do get hurt.

It's also unwise to set up this kind of aggressive physical relationship with boys because of what can happen later. All the fathers I've spoken to whose boys are now pretty much grown up report a stage in mid-teens where the boys seem to come at them like rutting stags or young gorillas for no particular reason – some primeval memory, perhaps, of challenging the alpha male's strength and authority. Having witnessed one of these challenges, which started out as playful wrestling but could have ended in the Old Bailey with one of them up on a murder charge had I not intervened, my advice would be for fathers to walk away when they sense a challenge brewing and discuss it later.

Father Work's most recent Christmas edition highlighted the work of the artist Caroline Mackenzie who had produced a 'father friendly' crib. In her nativity scene, Joseph is holding the baby Jesus, whilst Mary takes a rest after the birth. After two thousand years of patriarchal Christian history, the father finally gets a look in on the domestic front! The magazine also unpicks some of the less reliable, but highly publicised 'scientific research' about fatherhood. In the summer 2002 edition under the headline 'Myth Buster', the question was raised. 'Is being a home dad bad for your health?':

'You may believe, having read the papers recently, that being a "househusband" could send you to an early grave. Researchers had found, it was alleged, that the pressures of staying home to look after children significantly increased a man's risk of heart disease and early death. The US study found that men who described themselves as househusbands had an 82 per cent higher ten year death rate than men who worked outside the home.

Dr Elaine Eaker of Eaker Epidemiology Enterprises in Wisconsin who conducted the study said: "These findings may indicate that people who perform work or social roles incongruent with what is socially expected suffer greater heart disease and death." The men might feel pressure to "prove themselves" more than women looking after children, she added.

But is all this a lot of nonsense? Very possibly. Because, if you read the report closely, the study of home dads did not take into account one crucial factor: social class. It did take into account men's age, blood pressure, weight, diabetes and smoking habits. But not class.

Yet we have known for a long time that socially disadvantaged men die earlier. We also know that many – though certainly not all – men labelled "househusbands" are socially disadvantaged and unemployed, possibly because of long-standing illness or other problems. So it is hardly surprising that their life expectancy is lower on average than for men in general.

In short, the study proves little, except the willingness of some to believe that role reversal is inherently dangerous.'

In spring 2003 O'Sullivan embarked on a new and ambitious project together with Peter Howarth, a former editor of *Esquire*, who runs a company called Show Media. The new project is another glossy magazine, but this time intended for expectant and new fathers. Called *Dad*, it is described by the editors as 'first and foremost a men's magazine, but for dads – entertaining but informative in a low key way'. It has interviews with celebrity dads, such as Pierce Brosnan, and, predictably, David Beckham, and shows gadgets, fashion and cars – a feature on the five best pushchairs was shot by a car photographer and it was observed in a review that 'if the pictures were of Porsches instead of prams, it wouldn't look out of place in *Esquire*'.

Howarth's agenda is said to be the production of a magazine he would like to read himself. O'Sullivan is keen, as always, to raise awareness of the benefits of paternal involvement and to give young men who would be reluctant to pick up *Mother and Baby* or Penelope Leach the kind of information that every new parent, male or female, needs in order to move from crass amateur to practised professional without their guinea pigs – their first children – suffering too much.

O'Sullivan argues that fathers who are supported at work make better employees, a view backed by research carried out by the Equal Opportunities Commission and the Department of Trade and Industry and by the majority of employers. It's significant that a large employer of males, such as Ford Motors, bought 2,000 copies of the first edition of *Dad* to distribute to its staff. The pilot edition has been distributed through newsagents, but will also be given, through the NHS, to expectant and newly delivered fathers in selected hospitals. From September 2003, the NHS distribution will go nationwide twice a year, with the potential to reach more than 600,000 new fathers.

Ian Birch, editor-in-chief at the magazine publishing company Emap, responsible for the lad mag *FHM*, said of *Dad* in a recent newspaper article:

> *'Men want to be excited and entertained, not educated. And they hate being patronised. While a lot more men are involved in the process of having children, they are still a minority, and I think a lot of them would feel embarrassed at the idea of walking around with a magazine for fathers.'*

Birch concedes though, 'When we first started thinking about *FHM* everybody said it couldn't work.'

FHM now sells 670,000 copies a month, but overall sales of the lad mags are falling. I suspect O'Sullivan and Howarth have their fingers on the pulse of the new male zeitgeist. As so many surveys have shown, older men never say they wish they'd spent more time at the office. Invariably, when asked, they do say they wish they'd spent more time with their children. As, I have to confess at times, do those of we women who've devoted ourselves to careers.

I feel no guilt whatsoever at having committed myself to being the family breadwinner, but I do regret some of the time I spent away from them, some of the things I missed and some of the influence I might have had which they have missed. In my kind of career, part-time work is not an option – you're either in it for the hours it takes or you're not, and I wasn't prepared to down size as Jack has done. But I could have taken on fewer extra commitments and made more of an effort to get home for teatime rather than 'networking' in the bar. From my perspective of a mother with almost grown children, the time they are with you passes in a lightning flash.

I detest the expression work/life balance, it's become such a cliché and seems to set parents at work against those who have elderly relatives to look after or those who'd just like a year off to do something different, but I wish I had made a little more effort to balance my time in favour of home than I did.

Unsurprisingly, the 'Seatonites' in the press had a field day taking the mickey out of *Dad*. It was, said one article, a publication aimed at 'smug' dad – the one who pays lip service to fatherhood at home and flaunts it as he wheels the latest designer buggy down the high street. It is, regrettably, one of the pitfalls of sticking your head above the parapet to be at the forefront of social change that you will inevitably get it shot off. Ask any woman who dares to call herself by the f-word (feminist!). It is a matter of fact (I know because the feminist guru Betty Friedan told me and she was there) that no woman ever burned her bra in protest at the Miss World contest in 1968, but the media persists in describing 'women's libbers' as 'bra-burning man-haters' – carefully designed to undermine the seriousness of the message. 'New man' and 'smug dad' are in the same category and should be steadfastly laughed off by any man who has the foresight to see that change is inevitable and positive.

I do think Jack is right in his assessment that there are many more fathers who are beginning to realise how much they and their children are missing if they don't make the effort to spend time together. Some of them are even beginning to stick their heads above that parapet. One of the most encouraging conversations I had during the research for this book was with Donald Gayle who, together with a fellow social work student, Andy Kearney, runs a project in Bolton, which they have called Saturday Fathers Together. Donald, now forty, is in the final year of a social work degree at Salford University. He has a diploma in counselling and came to this kind of work after running a drug centre, but he was not always such an upstanding member of the community.

Donald's early experience was not unusual for a young, working-class black male. He had two sons when he was in his late teens, split up from their mother and then had a second family of two daughters with another partner; the two boys are now seventeen and twenty-one and the girls seven and ten. It's obvious from our conversation that his life was turned round by the responsibility of his job at the drug centre – he is vehemently opposed to drugs of any kind: 'my expertise says don't do it' – and by his determination that his boys should not replicate his irresponsible behaviour as regards family life.

> 'I had my first son when I was very young and I was fearful he would do the same. Neither of them [my sons] has and some of it may be down to the impact of seeing me change from Jack the Lad to responsible father. It's hard to really determine the impact, but I think I've taught them to have respect for women, to keep away from drugs and to know what it is to have a good father. I've always taught them that cannabis is the gateway to hard drugs and I've taught them everything about the dangers of experimentation – I've even threatened to test them, I'm so paranoid about it. I wouldn't test them. I don't think it's my place to infringe their human rights, but I hope I can trust them. I'm always amazed at parents who aren't on top of it. I know parents whose sons go up to their bedrooms, sniffing substances, and the parents think they're up there clearing up. You have to keep sitting down and talking with them.'

The Saturday Dads project came out of a conversation with Andy about the difficulties faced by fathers who are separated from their children. They managed to get funding, hired a small room and were inundated with men wanting help. After they set up a website and appeared on Radio 4's *Home Truths*, they found there was interest in what they were doing from all over the country:

> 'There's no support system at all for males. I won't downplay those dads who are dangerous to their partners and their kids – they shouldn't be allowed the kind of access that puts women and children at risk. I appreciate there are some fathers who should never get their kids, but most aren't like that. But so many fathers don't have a clue, because they never thought they needed to know how to bring up children. So when relationships break up, they go

through the court, they're granted some contact, often supervised, and have to prove they are capable of looking after a child and it's a minefield.

We are a small charity and we look at small things. We provide a place where dads can come with their kids and have someone around to talk to and help out when necessary. We get referrals from the social services and we check out the history of anyone who comes. Some I know are only there because the court has told them to come. There's always a key holder and a volunteer there and we try to be informal, but people sign in and sign out. We have to keep control. We're not able to do fully supervised contact, we haven't the resources. So we would take on a man who was considered low risk – he might have been involved in verbal abuse and arguments and hasn't had contact for some time, but we wouldn't take anybody who was considered high risk – anyone who'd been involved in physical violence.

We've got a few facilities like a computer, a TV, a video and a games console, but the most important work we do, I think, is giving fathers the chance to talk about how much the culture and the social environment have changed and how to fit into it. We talk about how women no longer do what women of the '60s and '70s did and we have to acknowledge that. I talk about how I've pushed a pram and changed a nappy and raise some of the difficulties for a man of being involved with his children. I can remember when my son was fourteen or fifteen and he was ill. He jumped into bed with me and put it in his school diary. I was really nervous, wondering if somebody read it, what would they think?

It's especially hard to know what to do about daughters. One bloke let his daughter wash his hair in the bath. One of his neighbours threatened to tell the social services. Some men don't even want to bath their daughters over a certain age because they worry about how it will be construed. One guy, who had weekend access, has a daughter who got nappy rash. The mother accused him of abuse and took the child to hospital. It was all checked out by the social services and they concluded the child had nappy rash.

Another, who had a son, wasn't allowed to go to see his boy play in the quarter final of a football cup match because the mother was going to be there. It's often the case that the dads miss out on school plays and such like sometimes because the school has no way of informing them about what's going on. The parent who doesn't have the child living with them isn't on the school contact form unless they make the effort to do it themselves. So they don't even get consulted when there are problems. And the mothers are so fed up and angry – sometimes with good cause if he's been a dad who never bothered till they split up – they're never going to want to tell them anything.

When all this is going on, if a bloke's on his own, he thinks he's the only one in the world. In the group they realise these problems are shared and they can discuss all sorts of things like getting an education, looking for a job and dealing with the Child Support Agency. One hundred per cent of our fathers now realise that it is their job to pay their way for their children. Some of them do need educating that they must contribute and that the welfare of the child is the most important thing. We try to help them understand that divorce and separation are like bereavement. Parents think it won't affect the child, but it does, you see their behaviour change. And if they are being poisoned from one side or the other they get very depressed.

As well as the informal discussions where these kinds of things get aired we run a parenting skills course for the fathers. It's two hours long and very intensive and covers stuff like basic health – how to brush a child's teeth for instance. We talk about emotional warmth. How it's OK to hug and cuddle your child. Most men have always relied on women to do it. We discuss boundaries and how to set them and advise them not to buy things for the kids that the mother will see as spoiling. The aim is not to alienate the mother, but help her. We say don't buy a Play station, buy a pair of shoes. Be a father, not a bank. It makes them think about what their child thinks of them and what they want their child to think of them.

We also try and teach basic cooking skills and tell them to keep away from MacDonald's – the sad Saturday dad's last resort. We encourage them to learn the kind of skills their sons need to see them using. Getting the ironing board out, for instance, when the lad is there, so he sees it's Dad doing it, not Mum.

As I said, we're a small charity and we look at the small things and we do have successes – they're small too, but really important. It's great when one of the dads reports back on a disagreement with his son and says, "I didn't shout at him, I talked to him", or when one of the kids comes in and says, "Me dad ironed me shirt", or another lad says, really proudly, "Me and me dad's 'ad chips and we didn't go to't chippy. They were chips that me dad 'ad made". It might not seem much, but it's a start and it's a big step for some of these men who've never thought they had to cook a thing in their lives.'

Donald's experiences send out a powerful wake-up call to men and women. We have to teach our boys the basic skills that the men in his group are picking up far too late – when their relationships have already broken down. But women need to hear, too, that feminism's fight with men has to move into a ceasefire. I'm not talking about those men who murder their wives, children and sometimes kill themselves after a bitter break up. Where there has been violence against women and/or children in a family there should be no access until a man can prove he is not a danger to them. There is pressure at the moment from an all-party parliamentary group for the government to adopt just such a law. Similar legislation works well in New Zealand.

But the majority of men are simply lost and floundering for a role. Women need to recruit good, open-minded men to the cause of equality if we are to reap the rewards of the feminist struggle. As Richard Reeves suggests in a chapter headed 'Patriarchy to Paternity' in his powerful paper for the Work Foundation, *Dad's Army – the Case for Father-Friendly Workplaces*: 'to move forward it is important – as one of the contributors to the Work Foundation Seminar argued – to create "no blame" conversations. We are where we are; and everyone's losing out. The key is to find ways forward.'

Thus men need to be more proactive about what they want out of their family life, rather than reacting to what's expected of them or simply opting for the traditional, easy choice. Women need to be less proprietorial about the raising of children and the quality of domestic work. You can't expect a father to be beating down the door to take over the childcare if you constantly accuse him of incompetence in changing a nappy, low standards of cleanliness (in this I am guilty as charged!) and not bringing in enough for that exotic holiday.

Richard Reeves is another young man who has worked tirelessly to influence public policy and achieve changes in the way the workplace operates to enable fathers to make choices about the way they want to work. In an article for the *Observer* newspaper he wrote in response to Sylvia Ann Hewlett's book *Baby Hunger*, which painted a depressing picture of high-flying women whose biological clocks are winding down, torn between their public success and their private grief at denying themselves a family.

'Male baby hunger is not as great as women's – few have to make such a stark choice between reproduction and professional success. Baby peckishness, perhaps. But it is real, nonetheless. It is not socially acceptable for them to say, but men do ache for children – their own, all too often – and they do want to spend more time being Dad. "Spending more time with the family" is still seen as code for professional failure for men, rather than a real desire.

The entry of women into the workplace should be freeing men. It should mean that breadwinning and caring can be shared. What is actually happening is that successful women are being forced either to ape male working patterns and forgo children or pay a mummy career penalty, while men remain as firmly caught in the breadwinner trap as ever.

In real life there is no Superman or Superwoman. There are ordinary people trying to make the best of things. And right now, both men and women are living shallower lives because of our collective failure to abandon our moribund models of masculinity, motherhood and success. Men want children to feature more strongly in their lives, but are stuck at the office. Women want to use their talents in the workplace, but get stuck with the kids or end up without them.

If men and women begin to see that their struggles are two sides of the same coin; if together they demand real changes in working culture and legislation; if "working father" becomes a meaningful term – then we might all live better and more balanced lives. Right now we are all hungry.'

There is some indication that campaigners like Jack and Richard are having some success in bringing about cultural change. Significant numbers of major employers are openly admitting that they get a better job from employees who are content with their lot and, even though Britain still works the longest hours in Europe, there does seem to be a growing awareness among employers that long hours are not necessarily productive.

In April 2003 the government introduced a law which was greeted with scepticism in some quarters, but goes a long way to satisfying the demands of campaigners like Richard and Jack. Patricia Hewitt, the Trade and Industry Secretary was responsible for this shift in policy. The new law gives fathers the right to two weeks' paternity leave – paid. Upwards of 360,000 fathers each year are expected to take up the offer. Even more important is the right, equal to that offered to mothers, for the fathers of children under the age of six, or up to eighteen if the child is disabled, to ask for flexible working.

This could mean job sharing, working longer hours, but for only four days a week or what's known as 'annualising', which means working intensely for busy periods and taking longer breaks at home with children. At the moment the number of fathers with young children who are working flexibly reaches barely 15 per cent and only 3 per cent have a job share. One in eight working fathers put in sixty hours a week and more than a third work more than forty-eight hours a week.

It is, of course, only a beginning. Laws don't effect cultural change, but they do signal a political will to help it come about. Employers will be able to refuse flexible working if they can make a good business case for their refusal, and six is still very young in a child's life to make a cut-off point. But it is a start. It's what the political commentator, Jackie Ashley, in an article in *The Guardian* in March 2003, called 'A Law that Could Change Everything'. She quotes the research I've outlined above, which shows the benefits to boys of having good fathers around in keeping them interested in education, succeeding in exams and away from crime, and she concludes:

'There are big social questions left to be discovered through this permissive legislation. It could be the wettest of damp squibs or it could be genuinely revolutionary. It all depends on the reaction of the rest of us. Do we want less dysfunctional kids and better skilled young adults? Are we prepared to put in the earlier investment and to accept the hassle and negotiation needed for fathers to be proper fathers? Or, in twenty years' time, are we still going to be wringing our hands and bleating about vandalism, street violence and "disappointing" school results? In the end, this isn't about "working practices". It is about civilisation.'

I couldn't have put it any better myself.

CHAPTER EIGHT

OEDIPUS SCHMOEDIPUS

You remember I've been saying throughout this book that my main aim in writing it was first to celebrate the sons we have and then to try and encourage other parents to help the next generation of young men to grow up with the skills and attitudes required to make a first rate husband or partner and hands-on father. No more Allerednic Syndrome, no more relationships stretched on the rack of mismatched expectations, no more boys and men who think it's OK to abuse a woman physically, mentally or verbally or who think manhood means dominating or excluding women. In short, no more raising a man who will be a rod for some poor woman's back.

I stand by every word. But . . . let me tell you how tough it is suddenly to realise you put in all that hard work and unconditional devotion for half your life, for heaven's sake, and all for some other lucky woman's benefit! During the writing of this book, after years of having lots of girl friends and, I suppose, the occasional flutter, but nothing to write home about and certainly no-one significant enough to bring to meet the parents, my son, Edward, fell in love.

I suppose, as he's just had his twentieth birthday, it would be a little strange if by now he hadn't embarked on a grand passion, and I would be frantic with worry if he had no-one to care for him and make him happy now he's away at university, but nothing had prepared me for the heart wrenching sense of no longer being the most important woman in his life. It isn't me he'll turn to when he's sick. It's her. It isn't me he'll need to fill out the forms he finds such a bore. It's her. He won't snuggle up to me on the sofa when his back is aching, looking for a cuddle and a massage. His triumphs, his tragedies, his worries, his intimacies – I will no longer be his first port of call when he needs to share them. This is jealousy, abandonment and desolation on a scale never before imagined.

I used to wonder why my mother-in-law – mother of five sons – never seemed to have a good word to say about any of the women they hooked up with. She was never openly hostile to my face, but I knew from what she let slip about all the others that I couldn't possibly escape behind my back. No-one was good enough for her precious boys. I used to accuse her (behind her back, of course) of suffering from what I called the Mrs Morel Syndrome – the mother in D. H. Lawrence's *Sons and Lovers* – who I used to characterise as a bitter, twisted old bat, disappointed in her marriage and hanging on to her sons like a sorry limpet. Now, I'm afraid I have every sympathy. In fact I'm in the throes of an acute case.

The mother-in-law from hell of popular imagination and familiar from the 'comedy' routines of the likes of Les Dawson or Bernard Manning is generally the mother of the bride – 'Behind every successful man stands a proud wife and a totally flabbergasted mother-in-law' Ba boom! 'My mother-in-law gave me two sweaters for Christmas. I wore one. "What's the matter?", she says, "You didn't like the other one?"' Ba boom! '"Excuse me, sir, your mother-in-law has died, do we bury her or cremate her?" "Do both, take no chances!"' Ba boom! And my personal favourite: 'Wife: Darling you hate all my relatives. Husband: No I don't hate all your relatives. In fact, I love your mother-in-law better than mine.' Ba ba boom!

I could only find one joke that seems to tell it like it really it is: 'A man was late home and his wife spotted a grey hair on his coat. Her eyes flashing, she screeched at him, "You've been at your mother's again, getting sympathy!"'

I'm not proud of falling so alarmingly into this dreadful stereotype and I might have begun to be anxious about my motives – is this middle-aged madness, is there something perverted about this passion for one's first-born son? – had I not spoken to others in the same position. I've concluded yet again what I suspected in the first chapter of this book. For a mother her son is half herself and half the man with whom she chose to breed. The Holy Grail, the perfect male. No wonder we're so heartbroken at losing him!

One friend told me of a pal of hers who's a lone parent of a single son. He had just gone off to university. She had endured that awful period we all go through when the sound of wings flapping as they ready themselves to fly the nest is deafening and now, for the first time, the umbilical cord was stretched to breaking point. How long, she was asked, was it since he had gone? 'Five days, three hours and twenty-six minutes,' came the reply and there wasn't even, yet, another woman involved.

Clare Wigzell went through it all with her son, George, who, when he was sixteen, had a serious relationship which lasted for a year.

'His girlfriend's mother was a single parent and I think the girl didn't feel comfortable in our busy, noisy household. So George spent all his time over there. She wouldn't come here. I lost him for a whole year. I would drive him over there and drop him off, then turn the car around towards home and cry all the way. He didn't speak to me any more. "Why would I want to talk to you?" he would say, "It's embarrassing." I went through an awful lot of grief because I was so completely cut out of his life. Of course, I'm the adult and I had to tell myself it's not his issue, it's mine, but the grief and the loss were terrible.

I didn't push it at all, I knew I had to let him go or risk losing him altogether and he did come back to me. I do think there's something about mothers and sons that doesn't exist with daughters. None of my friends who have girls have described anything like what you and I have experienced. That feeling when George was a baby of being totally in love. I remember about three days after he was born shaking with love. It was so intense, it was almost like a physical attack. With Elliott it was a much gentler feeling. I had a big attack of fear over the thought of splitting my love between Elliott and George, but I think in retrospect it was very lucky for George that we had another child to take some of that intensity away.

We do invest so much of our emotional life in our children and it felt to me when George invested so much in his girlfriend my emotional life was gone.

That doesn't seem to happen with daughters. A level of emotional intimacy seems to remain with them, but boys do seem to find it difficult and for the mother it's quite a problem.

I'm a very independent and busy person and you know you have to get over it, because it's not their problem and I don't think I'll ever feel the intensity of that jealousy again. He has a new girlfriend now and she fits in with us much more easily. She likes being here in our family life, so that makes things much better. But I'm not free of it altogether. For his A level English, he had to do a coursework exercise where he had to change one medium into another. He chose to adapt part of Marge Piercy's novel Woman on the Edge of Time *into a radio play. Now I gave him that novel. It's one of those books that "changes lives" and it changed mine and it changed his. It thrilled him and turned him on to literature. And when he finished the piece of work he showed it to me proudly and the dedication was to his girlfriend. Can you imagine how much that hurt! So I'm not out of danger yet!'*

Jenny Stephen was quite shameless in her 'confessions-of-a mother-in-law-from-hell-in-waiting'.

'I don't think I've ever been jealous of my sons' girlfriends, but there was one I wasn't sure of, I suppose I didn't really like her, so I set her a few challenges. I quite deliberately engaged her in intellectual debate and another I took ski-ing. I taught her to ski and ran her lessons like a boot camp to test her mettle. The question for me is always, "If this girl marries my son, will he have an interesting life?" Obviously a mother can't make their decisions for them, but you can demonstrate there might be a mismatch and hope they'll spot it.'

For Lynne Segal, one of her disappointments is that her son, Zim, doesn't yet, at the age of thirty-three seem to have found a soul mate, although I wonder if her absence of any jealousy can only come when the boy has been out of the nest for some time. Maybe she forgets what it was like when the separation was still raw.

'I like "losing" my son to another woman, especially as those other women have so far always been extremely nice to me. I only worry, and a very great deal, when he does not have another woman to love and be loved by.'

Richard Denton was pragmatic and resigned.

'I think I would be less jealous of my son bringing home a girlfriend than I will be when my daughter brings home a boyfriend. I really don't want to think about them leaving. The trouble is with kids, you devote twenty to thirty years to raising them all and they just piss off. As we did. My poor mother, I went off to university and didn't even call her for ten weeks. I guess it's pay back time.'

India Knight and Jackie Kay have some way to go before they have to face this question. India is a little nervous, 'I have strong Peggy Mitchell tendencies, but hopefully they'll have been curbed by the time my boys get hitched.' And Jackie, when asked what kind of mother-in-law she expected to be, answered, 'A relieved one.' Maybe, eventually I too will come round to feeling glad to have been let off the responsibility hook, I just can't quite see it yet.

A recent article in *Weekend* magazine about children of the feminist revolution talked to two young men who had been raised acording to some of the principles I'm advocating here. Jake Lushington, a thirty-four-year-old TV producer, was revealing about his experience of other men.

'Being raised by my mother I think I was given a good education about women. What I had to learn about more as an adult was masculinity. When I was at school I'd go out to the pub with the lads, but now I tend to avoid large gatherings of heterosexual men. My closest male friend is gay, but I have other close friends who are straight. I find their company fine when it's just two of us together or maybe a group of three. My only recent experience of a big male group was a stag night, which involved the most boring conversation I've ever had. Fifteen minutes of talk about anal sex I can find mildly diverting, but three and a half hours? No.'

Reuben Cohen is twenty-seven, a book publicist and writer. He spoke about his relationships with women.

'All my partners have been very independent, but not necessarily political. I've been involved with two women who would describe themselves as feminists, but only one in an organised way. I suppose the main impact of my upbringing is that I've been drawn to women who read a lot and care about books and can hold their own in conversation. It may not sound like much, but I think it's significant.

There's no question for me that feminism is more necessary now than ever. My mother has been quite taken aback by how things have turned out, I think. She describes her female students as highly intelligent and very confident in ways that young women of her generation weren't. Still, though, she has a sense that there's something missing.

Obviously there was no greater testament to the necessity of some gender consciousness than Bridget Jones's Diary. I think it proved, beyond doubt, that sexual politics do matter.'

Sweet music to my ears – a mother's influence does penetrate and in these two cases, at least, seems to have been entirely to the good.

Going back for a moment to this question of my acute case of Mrs Morel Syndrome. I have explained it to Ed, and not just because he needed to know if I was going to write about it in the book, but because it seemed to me he needed to understand what I was feeling, that I was grappling with it, that it was not his problem, but mine and that it had nothing to with any of the personalities involved. He has shown himself to be what I always hoped – kind, honest, open, loving, honourable and incredibly adept at steering his way through the battlefield of family life with tact, diplomacy and affection. More able, in fact, than I have been. I can't deny there have been moments when my behaviour has been, subconsciously I hope, designed to induce an element of guilt.

I learned, you see, long ago that you don't have to be Jewish to be a Jewish mother. I have been pushy and demanding and I doubt

I'll ever be off their case. 'You didn't call?' 'You got a 2.1 – why not a 1st?' In an emergency I'll be the one crying, 'My son, the vet/doctor/lawyer/Nobel laureate, is drowning.' You see, that's what I may well have been doing throughout this tome – simply shouting out my sons' achievments for the purposes of self-aggrandisement. But then, what's left when, as Richard so eloquently put it, they just 'piss off'. I hold to my heart the wise words of Jewish mothers everywhere, *'Oedipus schmoedipus* – who cares, so long as he loves his mother?' and I trust, guys, you always will.

Bibliography and Further Reading

Biddulph, Steve, *Raising Boys* (Thorsons, 2003)

Cooper, Al (ed.), *Sex and the Internet* (Brunner Routledge, 2003)

Elsa Ferri, John Bynner and Michael Wadsworth, (eds), *Changing Britain Changing Lives* (Institute of Education, University of London, 2003)

Formaini, Heather, *Men – the Dark Continent* (Mandarin, 1991)

Jenning, Charles, *Fathers' Race* (Little, Brown & Co, 1999)

Kahn, Tim, *Bringing up Boys* (Piccadilly, 1998)

Wayne Martino, and Bob Meyenn, (eds), *What about the Boys?* (Open University Press, 2001)

Maushart, Susan, *Wifework* (Bloomsbury, 2001)

Miller, Andy, *Tilting at Windmills* (Penguin Viking 2002)

Phillips, Angela, *The Trouble with Boys* (Pandora, 1993)

Roche, Lauren, *Life on the Line* (Zymurgy Publishing, 2003)

Skelton, Christine, *Schooling the Boys* (Open University Press, 2001)

Stubbs, Marie, *Ahead of the Class* (John Murray, 2003)

Taylor, Laurie and Matthew, *What are Children For?* (Short Books, 2003)

Tooley, James, *The Miseducation of Women* (Continuum, 2002)

Turner, E. S., *Boys will be Boys* (Michael Joseph, 1947)

Weeks, Jeffrey, *Sex Politics and Society* (Longman, 2000)

INDEX

Buy Vermilion Books

Order further Vermilion titles from your local bookshop, or have them delivered direct to your door by Bookpost

Is it me, or is it hot in here?
by Jenni Murray   0091887771   £6.99

FREE POSTAGE AND PACKING
Overseas customers allow £2.00 per paperback

BY PHONE: 01624 677237

BY POST: Random House Books
c/o Bookpost, PO Box 29, Douglas
Isle of Man IM99 1BQ

BY FAX: 01624 670923

BY EMAIL: bookshop@enterprise.net

Cheques (payable to Bookpost) and credit cards accepted

Prices and availability subject to change without notice.
Allow 28 days for delivery.
When placing your order, please mention if you do not
wish to receive any additional information.

www.randomhouse.co.uk